Learn Python Using Soccer

Table of Contents

Table of Contents 2

Free Gift 3

Disclaimer 4

Importance of Programming 5

Why Python? 8

Why use Soccer for Python? 10

Installing Python 12

Your First Python Programs 17

Python Variables 24

Printing Data onto a Screen in Python 37

Python Conditionals 41

User Input in Python 48

Learn Loops Using Soccer 53

Basic Math in Python using Soccer 62

Arrays in Python 80

Lists in Python 90

Drawing in Python 99

Moving a Soccer Ball on the Screen 121

Practice Test 132

Conclusion / Next Steps 143

Free Gift

We do want you to succeed in coding. To ensure your success, we are giving you a free list of projects that you can work on once you are completed with this book.

https://coding.gr8.com/

Disclaimer

Copyright © 2023

All Rights Reserved.

No part of this book can be transmitted or reproduced in any form including print, electronic, photocopying, scanning, mechanical or recording without prior written permission from the author.

While the author has taken utmost efforts to ensure the accuracy of the written content, all readers are advised to follow information mentioned herein at their own risk. The author cannot be held responsible for any personal or commercial damage caused by information. All readers are encouraged to seek professional advice when needed.

Importance of Programming

It was a bright Sunday afternoon, and Lily decided to spend quality time with her daughter, Amy.

They eagerly opened the DIY Robotics kit that they had bought on Amazon. As they assembled the robot, Lily noticed a very puzzled look on her daughter's face. Some of the instructions seem to be missing, and one of the components seemed faulty. Not sure what to do Lily called on her cousin, Steve. Steve was a young kid as well in the same school, but he had spent a few months learning programming. He had not touched a robot just like Amy. But Steve approached the situation differently. He looked up instructions for a similar robotic kit online, and then viewed a map of the different items on YouTube. He figured out which component was faulty and found a replacement part. With Steve's help, they continued with the task of building the robot.

Within a few hours, they completed the task with no issues. Steve's brief interaction with programming had improved his problem-solving skills by an immeasurable amount, and he was able to apply these principles to problems outside the computer screen.

Not only did Steve fix the robot, but he also ignited Amy's love for robotics, and Lily got to spend some bonding time with her daughter, Amy.

Now let's look at another example. James was a 10-year-old boy who dreaded doing his Math homework. His parents were worried about him falling behind the rest of the class and getting bad grades. They had tried a bunch of math tutors but none of them really seemed to help. None of them were able to hold James' attention. However, James had a passion for computer games, and he would spend hours playing them after school. James' uncle came up with the idea of teaching James how to program computer games to see if that would help James at school. James enrolled in a coding course which he attended every day after school. Even though James struggled initially, he grew to love the course. Over the weeks and months of the course, his problem solving and logical thinking improved tremendously. He was not only able to complete his homework, but he was also able to do it quickly. He was able to outcompete the rest of his class at Math and Physics, and also had learnt a skill that none of his classmates could do. And he had a lot of fun doing it.

Both James and Amy are good examples of how programming can change a kids' approach to solving a problem. The problem can be a Math problem, a physics problem, an engineering problem or even another programming problem. The logical approach to solving a problem can be used by anyone for the rest of their life, at school and at work.

In this book, we look to make programming a lot more fun using real world applications in the most popular sport in the world, and one of the fastest growing sports in the United States. We hope you have as much fun learning as we did from creating this book.

Why Python?

While the choice of whether to learn programming is not a difficult one, the choice of programming language is not that simple.

There are thousands of programming languages to choose from, and there are more being created every day. However, sticking to the most popular ones will yield the best results, as they have the most community support and online documentation.

The right programming language for you depends on what you are using it for. If you are looking to create high performance software applications and games, C++ would be the best choice. However, it is not recommended for beginners as it is a difficult program to learn.

If you're looking to create a website, Javascript is the best programming language as it integrates well with html and css elements.

However, the best programming language that is recommended for beginners is Python.

It is simple and readable. It is easy to read and write, which makes it ideal for beginners to start learning. Python can be used for a wide variety of applications, from web development to machine learning and scientific computing.

Python has a large helpful community around the web that helps beginners with answers to basic questions.

Python has a large and active community of developers, which means there is a wealth of third-party libraries and frameworks available. For example, Django and Flask are great libraries for web development, NumPy and pandas for data manipulation, and TensorFlow and PyTorch for machine learning.

Python is also an open-source program, which means it is free to use and modify without paying any licensing fees.

Python has excellent libraries like NumPy, Pandas, Schikit-learn etc. which make it the best language for data analysis and machine learning. As a result, Python programmers have a wealth of opportunities in the job market.

Why use Soccer for Python?

Anyone who's ever learnt programming knows that while it's really fascinating and interesting, it can get pretty difficult at times. It's tough when you get stuck on a certain problem and keep getting the same error. At times, it's a little tedious when you get to longer length programs.

It's important that you're programming on something that you're passionate about. It's tough when you're making generic "Hello World" programs like everyone else. That's why most people drop out of programming and never learn much.

That's the reason we came up with this topic for programming. Using soccer examples, we make coding a lot more interesting. However, if you're not interested in soccer, or don't like soccer, we don't recommend this book. This is mainly for soccer fans. You can check out our other books on Amazon.

Soccer is the most popular sport in the world, and among the fastest growing sports among the younger population in the US. We know we can inspire a huge population interested in this sport to get into programming and change their lives.

Most people have a basic knowledge of the rules and regulations of soccer. The familiarity can make it easier for beginners to grasp programming concepts. It can help increase engagement for those who are struggling through programming concepts. It makes programming less abstract and can bridge the gap between theory and practical learning.

Installing Python

Your first step in this journey is installing the Python program onto your computer.

Go to the website https://www.python.org/downloads/ and download the latest version of Python.

Windows Download

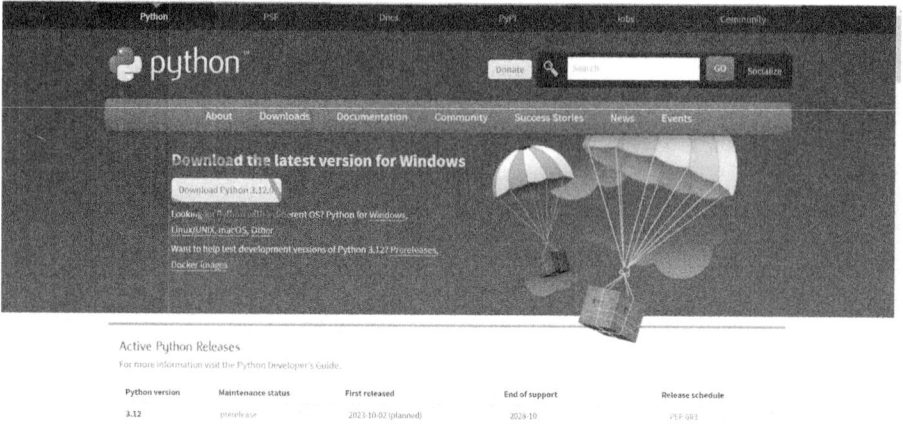

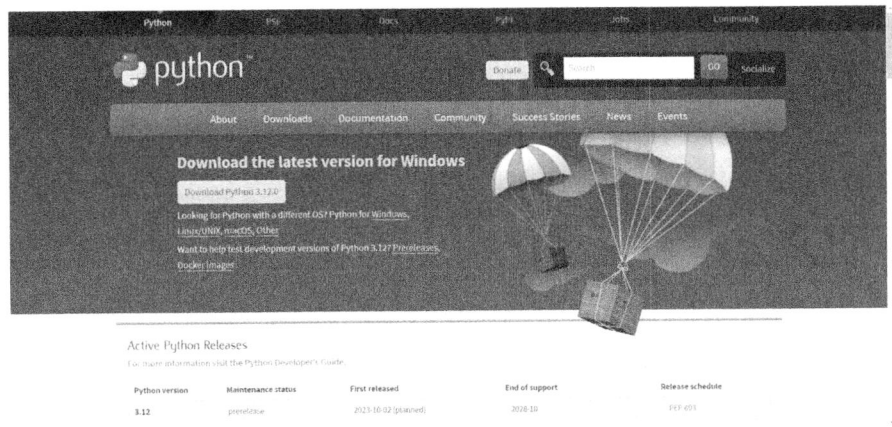

MAC Download

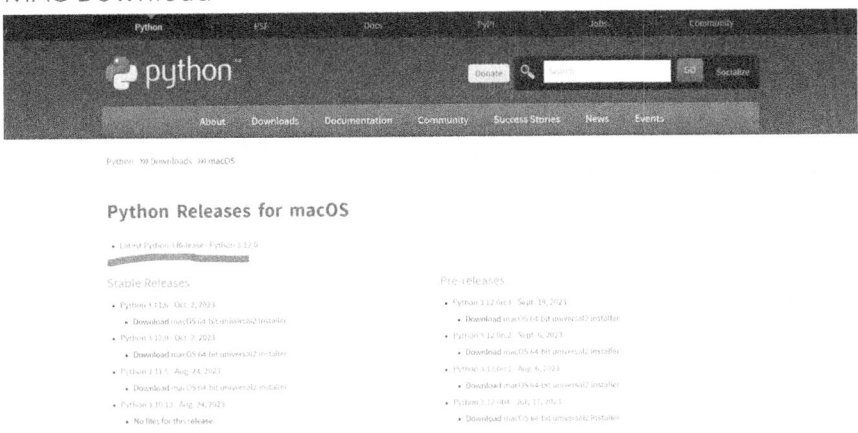

After downloading Python, install it on your computer as shown below.

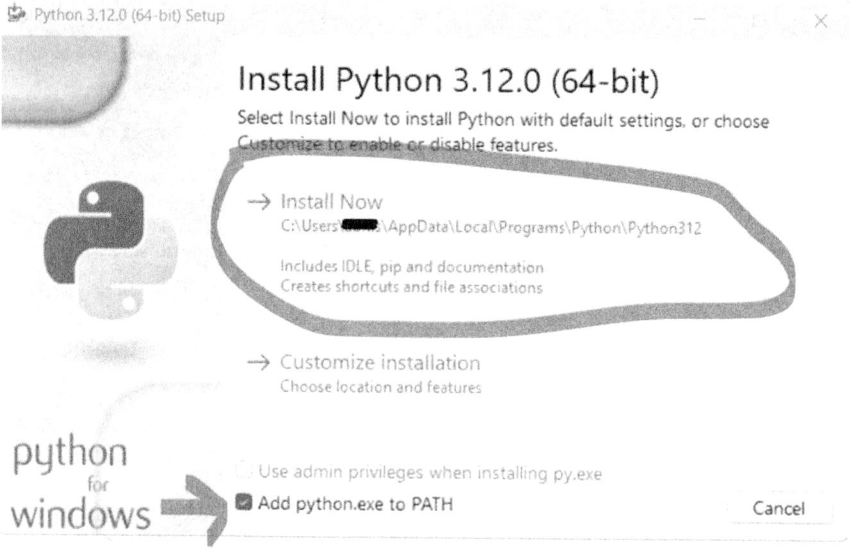

Install Python 3.12.0 (64-bit)

Select Install Now to install Python with default settings, or choose Customize to enable or disable features.

→ Install Now
C:\Users____\AppData\Local\Programs\Python\Python312

Includes IDLE, pip and documentation
Creates shortcuts and file associations

→ Customize installation
Choose location and features

☐ Use admin privileges when installing py.exe

☑ Add python.exe to PATH

Cancel

Text Editor

In this book, we will run Python on a text editor. Our preferred text editor is NotePad++.

Download the latest version at: https://notepad-plus-plus.org/downloads/ and install it.

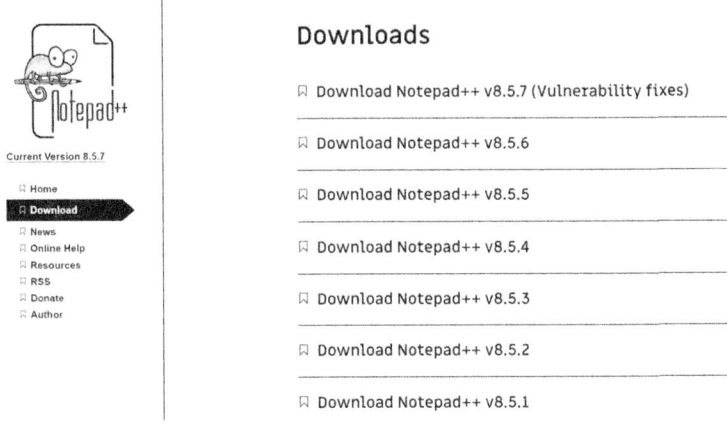

Once Installed, you can type in "Notepad++" in the TaskBar and open up NotePad++ as below:

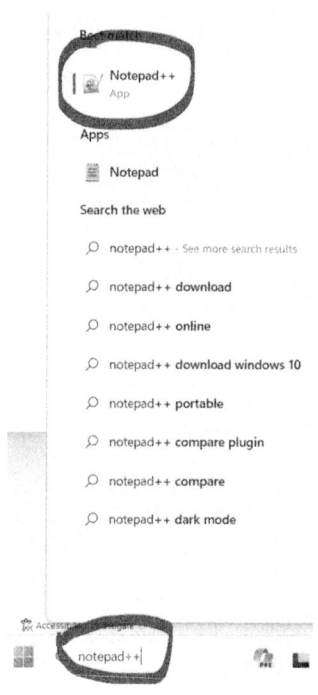

Your First Python Programs

In our first Python program, we will print the words "The beautiful game" onto the console screen.

First, open up **NotePad++.**

In NotePad++, type in **print("The beautiful game")** as shown below.

```
print("The beautiful game")
```

Now, save the file. Click "**File > Save As**".

Choose Python file in "Save As Type"

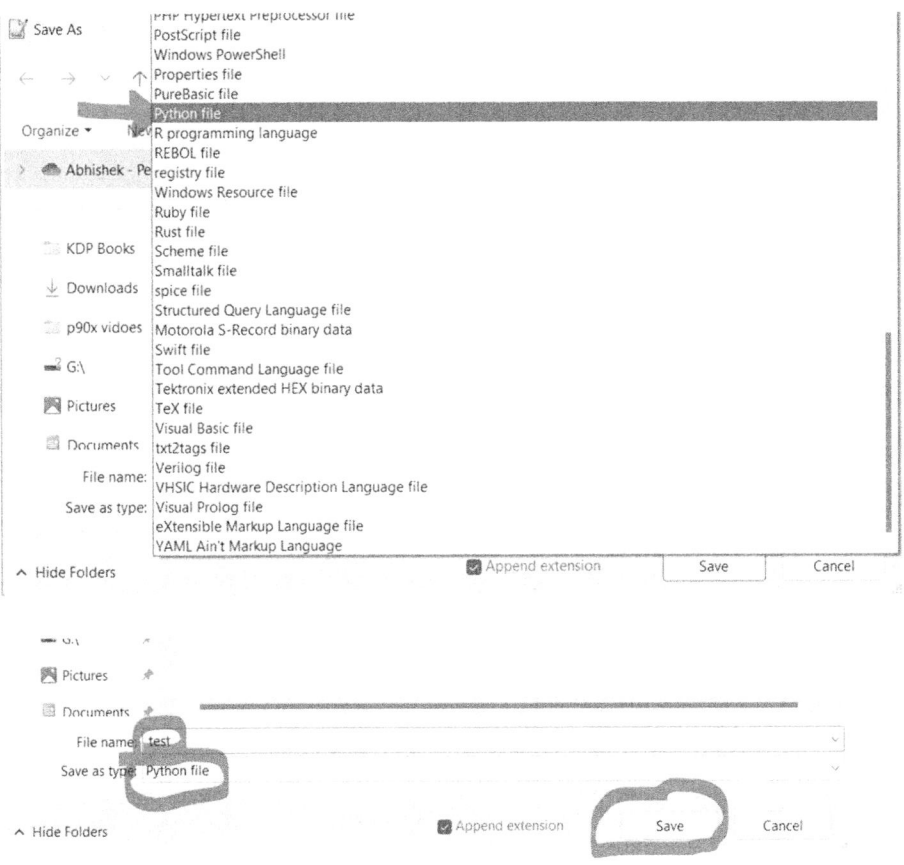

In this book, we are going to run all the files using Command prompt. To access **command prompt**, type in **cmd** in Taskbar search as shown below.

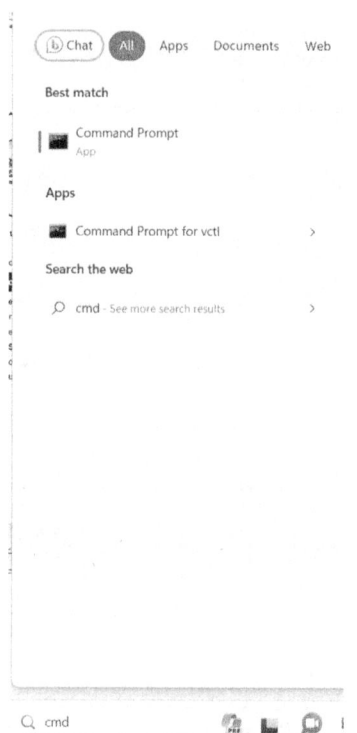

Browse to the correct folder in the user console. This path is going to be different for everyone based on where you saved the test.py file.

Once you get to the correct folder, run the program by typing in "python test.py"

And now you can see **"The beautiful game"** printed on the screen below.

Program 2

In the next program, we are going to print the sum of the numbers 4 and 5 on the screen.

Open up Notepad++ as before, and create a file called "test2.py" with 1 line. The line is print(4+5) as shown below.

Save the file.

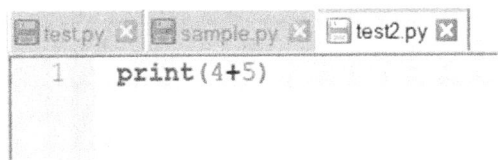

Run the program from Command console as shown below.

Once program is run, you can see the output of 9 on the screen.

```
C:\Users\____\python-programs>python test.py
The beautiful game!

C:\Users\____\python-programs>python test2.py
9
```

Exercises to Practice
1. Write a program that prints the word "Joga Bonito" on the screen.
2. Write a program that prints your favorite player's name on the screen.

Python Variables

A variable in programming is an item that stores a certain value. The value has to be a certain data type.

To describe it in soccer terms, a variable is like an equipment bag. A bag can store a certain type of equipment e.g. a round bag can only hold a soccer ball. A shoe bag can only hold soccer shoes. A soccer ball bag cannot hold shoes; and vice versa.

A variable can also change values within the program, as long as it's the same data type. So, we can replace the ball in a soccer bag and add a different one. Same thing with the equipment bag.

So, in programming, a variable is of a certain data type and holds a certain value. The value can change within the program. So, let's take the example of an integer variable **n**. An integer variable can only hold numbers.

```
int-variable.py
1    n=75
2    print("The value of n is ");
3    print (n);
```

And print the value of n:

```
C:\Users\___\python-programs>python int-variable.py
The value of n is
75
```

Now, let's change the value of variable **n** to 100.

```
1  n=75
2  print("The 1st value of n is ");
3  print (n);
4  n=100
5  print("The 2nd value of n is ");
6  print (n);
```

```
C:\Users\___s\python-programs>python int-variable.py
The value of n is
75

C:\Users\___>\python-programs>python int-variable-2.py
The 1st value of n is
75
The 2nd value of n is
100
```

Now, let's do the example of a string variable. A string variable holds a text character or a bunch of text characters.

Now, let's create a variable called **player1** which holds string "Ronaldo". Print out **player1** and we see that the program prints "Ronaldo".

```
player1="Ronaldo"
print("The value of player1 is ");
print (player1);
```

```
C:\Users\......\python-programs>python string-variable.py
The value of player1 is
Ronaldo
```

Now, let's change the value of variable **player1** to "Messi". Print out player1 again and see that the value of **player1** has changed to "Messi".

```
player1="Ronaldo"
print("The value of player1 is ");
print (player1);
player1="Messi";
print("The new value of player1 is ");
print (player1);
```

In Python, you don't need to specify the data type when declaring a variable. Python automatically detects the type based on what is stored inside the variable.

For example, when we put Player1 = "Ronaldo", Python makes Player1 a string variable based on the word" Ronaldo" being a string.

Python Variable Data Types

Now, let's look at the different data types used in Python.

1. **Integer Data Type int:** The integer data type is used to store whole numbers like 0,1,2 etc.

    In the example goals, the variables **team1goals** and **team2goals** hold the integer values of the number of goals scored by Team 1 and Team 2. These values are printed on the screen below.

```
1  team1goals=2
2  team2goals=5
3  print("Team 1 Goals:")
4  print(team1goals)
5  print("Team 2 Goals:")
6  print(team2goals)
```

Output:

```
Team 1 Goals:
2
Team 2 Goals:
5
```

2. **Float Data Type:** A float data type is used to store decimal numbers. In the example below, **player1_average_goals_per_game** and **player2_average_gaols_per_game** are two float variables that hold the decimal values of the average goals per game for the two players.

```
1  player1_average_goals_per_game=1.4
2  player2_average_goals_per_game=0.7
3  print("Player 1 Goals Per Game:")
4  print(player1_average_goals_per_game)
5  print("Player 2 Goals Per Game:")
6  print(player2_average_goals_per_game)
```

Output:

```
Player 1 Goals Per Game:
1.4
Player 2 Goals Per Game:
0.7
```

3. **String Data Type:** A string variable is used to store single non-numeric character/characters. In the example below, string variables **player1name**, **player2name** and **player3name** store the names of players as strings. These are all printed as outputs on the screen.

```
player1name="Salah"
player2name="Ronaldo"
player3name="Onana"

print("Player 1 Name:")
print(player1name)
print("Player 2 Name:")
print(player2name)
print("Player 3 Name:")
print(player3name)
```

Output:

```
Player 1 Name:
Salah
Player 2 Name:
Ronaldo
Player 3 Name:
Onana
```

4. **Boolean Data Type**: A Boolean variable is one that can hold two values. These two values are **true** and **false**. Boolean variables are used to perform checks, compare values of variables, compare names of variables etc.

   In the below example, there are two integer variables **team1goals** and **team2goals** that hold values of goals scored by team1 and team2.

   The Boolean variable **team1_win_boolean** compares the values of **team1goals** and **team2goals**. If team1goals is greater than team2goals, then **team1_win_boolean** returns a value of **true**. If not, it returns **false**.

   In the below example, team1goals is less than team2goals, so team1_win_boolean is **false**.

```
1   team1goals=2
2   team2goals=5
3   print("Team 1 Goals:")
4   print(team1goals)
5   print("Team 2 Goals:")
6   print(team2goals)
7
8   team1_win_boolean=(team1goals>team2goals)
9   print("Is it true that Team1 won")
10  print(team1_win_boolean)
```

Output:

```
Team 1 Goals:
2
Team 2 Goals:
5
Is it true that Team1 won
False
```

In the next example, there are two integer variables

player1_average_goals_per_game and

player2_average_goals_per_game that hold values of average goals per game scored by player1 and player2.

The Boolean variable **player_goals_per_game_better** compares the values of **player1_average_goals_per_game** and **player2_average_goals_per_game**. If **player1_average_goals_per_game** is greater than player2_average_goals_per_game, then **player_goals_per_game_better** returns a value of true. If not, it returns false.

In the below example, **player1_average_goals_per_game** is greater than **player2_average_goals_per_game**, so **player_goals_per_game_better** is **true**.

```
1  player1_average_goals_per_game=1.4
2  player2_average_goals_per_game=0.7
3  print("Player 1 Goals Per Game:")
4  print(player1_average_goals_per_game)
5  print("Player 2 Goals Per Game:")
6  print(player2_average_goals_per_game)
7
8  player_goals_per_game_better=(player1_average_goals_per_game>player2_average_goals_per_game)
9  print("Is it true that player1 scored more goals")
10 print(player_goals_per_game_better)
```

Output:

```
Player 1 Goals Per Game:
1.4
Player 2 Goals Per Game:
0.7
Is it true that player1 scored more goals
True
```

Sample Outputs:

To add 2 decimal numbers we would need to use the **float() data type as it would output an incorrect whole number. This is shown** below, as 5.1+6.2 would produce an answer of 11 if variable data type **int** was used.

```
>>> int(5.1+6.2)
11
>>> float(5.1+6.2)
11.3
```

If we want to join two strings together and print, then we need to use str() function as using int or float would produce an error.

```
>>> int("Steve "+"won")
Traceback (most recent call last):
  File "<stdin>", line 1, in <module>
ValueError: invalid literal for int() with base 10: 'Steve won'
```

```
>>> str("Steve "+"won")
'Steve won'
```

There are other data types like double, tuple, dict etc. but these are beyond the scope of this beginners' book.

Converting Between Data Types

Why would I need to convert data types?

In some cases, certain tasks in Python only can happen with certain data types. For example, if we want to print a string and an integer in the same line, we can't use **print("The winner horse is horse number"+5)**

It produces the error below.

```
>>> print("The winning horse is horse number" + 5)
Traceback (most recent call last):
  File "<stdin>", line 1, in <module>
TypeError: can only concatenate str (not "int") to str
```

We need to convert the number 5 to a string as shown below.

```
>>> print("The winning horse is horse number " + str(5))
The winning horse is horse number 5
```

If we want to work with whole numbers, then we need to convert all decimals to int using **int()**. For example **int(5.2)** would produce 5.

The following functions help to convert between data types.

str() converts any variable to a string data type

int() converts a variable into a integer data type

float() converts a variable into a float data type

Exercises to Practice

1. Create two integer variables called **manchesterunited** and **arsenal** and assign integer values to them equal to the number of goals scored in a match. Print out the values of each variable on the screen. Then, create a Boolean variable **compare_scores** to figure out who won the match, and print out the result using the value of the Boolean **compare_scores**.

2. Create two variables that store the average goals conceded by two goalkeepers. Print them on the screen. Then, create a Boolean variable **compare_averages** to figure out who is the better goalkeeper, and print out the result using the Boolean value.

3. Write a program that takes in two numbers and prints out their sum. The output message must be a combination of a string and a number. An example output would be "The sum of 2 and 5 is 7". The output statement would include the variables for 2,5 and 7.

Printing Data onto a Screen in Python

There are several ways to print data onto the screen in Python. For the purposes of this book we're going to go through 3 most commonly used ways to do so.

To demonstrate the differences in the 3 methods, we're going to print the line "Adam is 35 years old" on the screen in 4 different ways and each method is labelled on the screen.

```
1    print("Adam is 35 years old - 1st method")
2
3    name = "Adam"
4    age = 35
5
6    print(f"{name} is {age} years old - 2nd method")
7
8    print(name+ " is "+ str(age) + " years old - 3rd method")
```

1st Method: Normal Printing

In line 1, we print the entire line on the screen by putting it inside the print function. This is the simplest method and easiest way if we know the exact string that we want to print.

2nd Method: Printing using f-Strings

In the next method, we declare two variables **name** and **age**. In lines 3 and 4, name is a string variable assigned to **"Adam"** and age is an integer variable assigned to **35**.

In line 6, we use a method known as **f-string** printing which allows us to include variable names in the print string. The values of the variables replace the variable names when the output is printed on the screen. This method is invoked by starting the print string with the value f right before the double quotation.

This method allows us the flexibility to print the string even if the name and age variables are changed to different values.

3rd Method: Printing using String Concatenation

In this method, multiple strings are added together and input on the screen. They are added together using the "+" sign as shown in line 8. Since age is an integer variable, it has to be converted into a string using **str(age)** before being included in the output.

The outputs for all three methods are shown below:

Output:

```
Adam is 35 years old - 1st method
Adam is 35 years old - 2nd method
Adam is 35 years old - 3rd method
```

4th Method: Printing at End of String

If there's a string in which a variable need to be printed at the end of the string, we can use the comma operator to do so. See example below.

```
1    age = 35
2    print("Adam's age = ",age)
```

Output:

```
Adam's age =  35
```

Exercises to Practice

1. Create two variables **player1** and **player2** that hold the names of two soccer players Messi and Ronaldo. Create another two integer variables **goals1** and **goals2** that hold the goals scored by Messi and Ronaldo. Messi has 819 goals, while Ronaldo has 830 goals. Print out on the screen "Ronaldo has 830 goals" and "Messi has 819 goals". Use the first three methods listed above.
2. Print out "Argentina won the 2023 world cup" using the first three methods in the chapter.
3. Print out "Ronaldo's age = 38" using the 4th method in the chapter.

Python Conditionals

A conditional in programming is a way to perform a check to see if a certain condition is met. If a certain condition is met, it can perform a certain task. If it is not met, it can perform a different task. It is a very useful way to automate tasks and eliminate manual checks.

In the example below, the program has two integer variables **players_on_subs_bench** and **minimum_subs_required**. If the number of players (**players_on_subs_bench**) on the bench was greater than or equal to minimum subs (**minimum_subs_required**), then it prints a start match message on the screen. Else it prints out that there are not enough players to start the match.

players_on_subs_bench is assigned to a value of 1 in this program, and **minimum_subs_required** is assigned to a value of 5. Since **players_on_subs_bench** is the smaller value, it prints "Not enough players to start the match."

```
players_on_subs_bench = 1
minimum_subs_required=5

if players_on_subs_bench >= minimum_subs_required:
    print("Please start match.")
else:
    print("Not enough players to start the match.")
```

Output:

```
Not enough players to start the match.
```

Now, let's change the program to have more subs so it meets the conditions. **players_on_subs_bench** is changed to a value of 6. Since **players_on_subs_bench** is the larger value now, it prints "Please start match."

```python
players_on_subs_bench = 6
minimum_subs_required=5

if players_on_subs_bench >= minimum_subs_required:
    print("Please start match.")
else:
    print("Not enough players to start the match.")
```

Output:

```
Please start match.
```

Example 2:

The below program checks if the ball has crossed the goal line by checking exactly where the ball bounced. The integer variable **ballbouncepoint** stores the value of the ball bounce location.

If **ballbouncepoint** is greater than 700, it is judged to have crossed the line and goal is declared. If not, ball did not cross the line. No goal.

In below example, **ballbouncepoint** is below 700, so there is no goal printed as output on the screen.

```
1    ballbouncepoint = 600
2
3    if ballbouncepoint >= 700:
4        print("Ball crossed line. Goal!!")
5    else:
6        print("Ball did not cross line. No Goal!!")
```

Output:

```
Ball did not cross line. No Goal!!
```

In next example, **ballbouncepoint** is 750, which is more than the check of 700, so the output is **"Ball crossed line. Goal!!"** Goal is declared.

```
1  ballbouncepoint = 750
2
3  if ballbouncepoint >= 700:
4      print("Ball crossed line. Goal!!")
5  else:
6      print("Ball did not cross line. No Goal!!")
```

Output:

```
Ball crossed line. Goal!!
```

Example 3:

The below program checks the goals scored by team x and team y. These are stored in integer variables **team_x_score** and **team_y_score**. The team with the larger score wins. These are checked using if-else conditionals in lines 4-9.

If **team_x_score** is larger then **team_y_score**, then print "Team X wins". If **team_y_score** is larger than **team_x_score** then print "Team Y wins". If neither is true, then it goes to line 9 and prints **"It's a draw"**.

```
1    team_x_score = 1
2    team_y_score = 2
3
4    if team_x_score > team_y_score:
5        print("Team X wins!")
6    elif team_y_score > team_x_score:
7        print("Team Y wins!")
8    else:
9        print("It's a draw!")
10
```

Output:

In the first program, **team_y_score** is greater than **team_x_score**, so it prints "Team Y wins".

```
Team Y wins!
```

```
1    team_x_score = 3
2    team_y_score = 2
3
4    if team_x_score > team_y_score:
5        print("Team X wins!")
6    elif team_y_score > team_x_score:
7        print("Team Y wins!")
8    else:
9        print("It's a draw!")
10
```

In the next example, **team_x_score** is greater than **team_y_score**, so it prints "Team X wins".

Output:

```
Team X wins!
```

Team Winner

```python
team_x_score = 1
team_y_score = 1

if team_x_score > team_y_score:
    print("Team X wins!")
elif team_y_score > team_x_score:
    print("Team Y wins!")
else:
    print("It's a draw!")
```

In the next example, team_x_score is equal to team_y_score, so it prints "It's a draw".

Output:

```
It's a draw!
```

Exercises to Practice

1. Write a program that stores the number of substitutions in a variable and checks if it is less or more than 5. If the number is more than 5, print out that there are no more substitutions allowed. If it's less than 5, print out how many substitutions are left in the game.

2. Create two variables that contain the points received so far in the league for two teams that are playing a game. Write a conditional that checks the result of the game. If the game is a draw, both teams receive a point. If a team wins, the winner receives three points. Increase the value of the variables based on the result of the game.

3. Create two variables for goals scored and goals conceded for a team in the league. Calculate the goal difference for the team:

   goal difference = goals scored – goals conceded

   If the goal difference is above 0, print out that the team is performing below par, and if it's above 0, print out that the team is doing well.

User Input in Python

An important aspect of any programming language is the ability to accept data from the user while the program is running. This is called user input and is one of the most useful features of programming. With user input data, there is no need to change the data every time the variable value needs to be changed. Python is no different. In Python, we accept user input through the **input()** function, as shown below:

ui=input("Enter Anything:")

The words within the brackets on the input function are printed on the screen. So, **"Enter Anything"** is printed on the screen. The user now has the option to type something on the screen. Whatever the user types on the screen is stored in the variable **ui**.

Now, let's look at an example. In the program below, we ask the user to input their favorite soccer player, and print that on the screen. In line 1, the user inputs their favorite soccer player and it is stored in string variable **favp**. The default data type for a user input variable is a string.

In line 2, this is printed on the screen.

```
1    favp = input ("Who is your favorite soccer player?");
2    print("Your favorite soccer player is "+favp);
```

Output:

```
Who is your favorite soccer player?
```

```
Who is your favorite soccer player?Ronaldo
```

```
Who is your favorite soccer player?Ronaldo
Your favorite soccer player is Ronaldo
```

In the next example, the user inputs 2 separate values for goals scored and goals against and prints out the goal difference on the screen. The variables **goals1** and **goals2** store the user input variables for goals scored and goals conceded respectively. Since the default data type is string, both variables are converted to int before being stored. This is done so they can be used in line 3 as integers.

The goal difference is calculated in line 3 and stored in variable **goaldiff**.

In line 4, the value of **goaldiff** is printed on the screen. The required output for the print function is string, so the integer is converted to a string using **str(goaldiff)**.

```
1  goals1 = int(input ("Enter total goals scored: "))
2  goals2 = int(input ("Enter total goals conceded: "))
3  goaldiff=goals1-goals2
4  print("Team's Goal difference "+str(goaldiff))
```

Output:

```
Enter total goals scored: 15
Enter total goals conceded: 13
Team's Goal difference 2
```

```
Enter total goals scored: 12
Enter total goals conceded: 15
Team's Goal difference -3
```

```
Enter total goals scored: 10
Enter total goals conceded: 2
Team's Goal difference 8
```

Exercises to Practice

1. Write a program that takes in the value of your favorite soccer team and prints it on the screen.
2. Write a program that takes in the value of 15 players in your team and stores it in 15 different variables. Print out the names of only the starting 11 players at the end of the program.

Learn Loops Using Soccer

A loop in programming is a set of instructions that is repeated a fixed number of times.

In Python, a loop is declared as follows:

for x in range(a,b)

The above line has **x** as the counter of the loop, and it starts off with the value of **a**. The loop ends as soon as the counter x hits the value **b**.

In the first example below, the program prints out each penalty kick in a 30-kick penalty training session using a for loop.

The counter is the variable **kicks**. It starts with the number 1 and ends before it hits the number 31.

The penalty kick number is printed in each iteration of the loop, and the end of the session is printed after the loop is over in line 4.

Loop 1 Example: Penalty Kicks

```
1  for kicks in range(1, 31):
2      print("Finished Kick Number ",kicks)
3  print (" ")
4  print("End of penalty kick session")
```

Output:

```
Finished Kick Number  1
Finished Kick Number  2
Finished Kick Number  3
Finished Kick Number  4
Finished Kick Number  5
Finished Kick Number  6
Finished Kick Number  7
Finished Kick Number  8
Finished Kick Number  9
Finished Kick Number  10
Finished Kick Number  11
Finished Kick Number  12
Finished Kick Number  13
Finished Kick Number  14
Finished Kick Number  15
Finished Kick Number  16
Finished Kick Number  17
Finished Kick Number  18
Finished Kick Number  19
Finished Kick Number  20
Finished Kick Number  21
Finished Kick Number  22
Finished Kick Number  23
Finished Kick Number  24
Finished Kick Number  25
Finished Kick Number  26
Finished Kick Number  27
Finished Kick Number  28
Finished Kick Number  29
Finished Kick Number  30

End of penalty kick session
```

Loop 2 Example

The next program has a for loop that counts 5 substitutions for a team in a game.

```
1   for subs in range(1, 6):
2       print("Completed sub number ",subs)
3   print (" ")
4   print("No more substitutions left")
5
```

The for loop counter variable called **subs** takes on values from 1 to 5. The range(1, 6) function generates a sequence of numbers starting from 1 and ending at 5 (not including 6). So, **subs** will take on values 1, 2, 3, 4, and 5 in each iteration of the loop.

In each iteration of the loop, this line prints a message to the console. The message is a combination of a string ("Completed sub number ") and the current value of the subs variable, which represents the current iteration of the loop. This line will print messages like "Completed sub number 1," "Completed sub number 2," and so on, for each iteration of the loop.

After the loop is over in line 4, the programs prints that there are no more substitutions left for the team. This is seen in the output below.

Output:

```
Completed sub number 1
Completed sub number 2
Completed sub number 3
Completed sub number 4
Completed sub number 5

No more substitutions left
```

Example Loop 3: Fitness Training Session

In the next example, we create a loop that calculates the number of laps around a running track that a player does during a fitness training session.

In line 1, we create a variable **runningloops** that runs from 1 to 10 in a for loop. In each iteration of the loop, the program prints the lap number.

Once the loop is completed in line 4, the program prints that the running session is over for the player. This is seen in the output below.

```
1   for runningloops in range(1, 11):
2       print("Completed lap number ",runningloops)
3   print (" ")
4   print("Finishing running session")
```

Output:

```
Completed lap number  1
Completed lap number  2
Completed lap number  3
Completed lap number  4
Completed lap number  5
Completed lap number  6
Completed lap number  7
Completed lap number  8
Completed lap number  9
Completed lap number  10

Finishing running session
```

Loop Example: Nested Loops to count free kicks per training week.

In the next example, we explain the concept of a nested loop. A nested loop is just one loop within another.

A team has 3 training sessions per week, and 10 free kicks within each training session. To track and print each free kick in a training session, we create a loop with counter **weeklysessions** from 1 to 3. This is called the outer loop.

Each time the outer loop starts, we print the weekly session number in line 2.

Then, we create another loop within with the counter freekicks from 1 to 10. This is the inner loop. Within the inner loop, we print out the freekicks number, which helps keep track of the free kicks within each training session.

Once 10 freekicks are over, then the outer loop **weeklysessions** increases by 1 and we move back to line 2 to repeat the outer loop. And the process repeats till all weekly sessions are over.

Once all weekly sessions are over, the outer loop is over, and we print out that we have finished the weekly training session in line 6.

```
1  for weeklysessions in range(1, 4):
2      print("Weekly session: ", weeklysessions)
3      for freekicks in range(1, 11):
4          print("Completed free kick number ", freekicks)
5  print(" ")
6  print("Finishing weekly free kick training")
7
```

Output:

As seen in the output below, we print out 10 free kicks in each weekly session and then move on to next one. This continues till all 3 weekly sessions are over.

```
Weekly session:  1
Completed free kick number  1
Completed free kick number  2
Completed free kick number  3
Completed free kick number  4
Completed free kick number  5
Completed free kick number  6
Completed free kick number  7
Completed free kick number  8
Completed free kick number  9
Completed free kick number  10
Weekly session:  2
Completed free kick number  1
Completed free kick number  2
Completed free kick number  3
Completed free kick number  4
Completed free kick number  5
Completed free kick number  6
Completed free kick number  7
Completed free kick number  8
Completed free kick number  9
Completed free kick number  10
Weekly session:  3
Completed free kick number  1
Completed free kick number  2
Completed free kick number  3
Completed free kick number  4
Completed free kick number  5
Completed free kick number  6
Completed free kick number  7
Completed free kick number  8
Completed free kick number  9
Completed free kick number  10
Finishing weekly free kick training
```

Exercises to Practice

1. Build a Python program that simulates a workout session for a player with only 20 push ups. Print out the completion of each push up using a for loop.
2. Write a Python program that simulates 3 soccer training sessions. Each soccer training session has 20 free kicks, 10 penalty kicks, and 20 laps round the field.
   Hint: Use a nested loop with the outer loop that counts the number of training sessions. There are 3 inner loops that track free kicks, penalty kicks and laps.

Basic Math in Python using Soccer

Python is a great program to do basic math calculations. In this chapter, we'll look at basic programs that perform these operations.

Addition

Python does simple addition using the '+' sign. To illustrate with an example, we add the goals scored in 5 games and add them together.

Below program has 5 variables that holds the goals in 5 games. A 6th variable holds the sum of these 5 variables and prints it on the screen.

The 5 variables are **game1goals, game2goals, game3goals, game4goals** and **game5goals**. The variable **sumofgoals** in line 7 calculates the sum of these 5 variables and prints it on the screen.

The sum of all 5 variables in lines 1-5 is **8**, and this value is printed as an output on the screen.

```
1  game1goals = 1
2  game2goals = 0
3  game3goals = 2
4  game4goals = 0
5  game5goals = 5
6
7  sumofgoals = game1goals + game2goals + game3goals + game4goals + game5goals
8  print("Number of goals scored in 5 games")
9  print(sumofgoals)
```

Output:

```
Number of goals scored in 5 games
8
```

Subtraction

Python does simple subtraction using the '-' sign.

Below program has 2 variables that holds the total goals scored in a season, and total goals scored by Ronaldo. The program calculates the goals scored without Ronaldo. This is an important variable as Ronaldo is leaving at the end of the season. The variable **totalseasongoals** holds the total team goals, **ronaldogoals** holds total goals scored by Ronaldo.

A 3rd variable **estimated_goals_without_ronaldo** is the difference between the first 2 variables, and estimates the goals scored by the team without Ronaldo.

The difference of the two variables in lines 1-2 is **53** (85-32), and this value is printed as an output on the screen.

```python
totalseasongoals = 85
ronaldogoals = 32

estimated_goals_without_ronaldo = totalseasongoals - ronaldogoals
print("Estimated Goals Without Ronaldo")
print(estimated_goals_without_ronaldo)
```

Output:

```
Estimated Goals Without Ronaldo
53
```

Multiplication:

Python does simple multiplication using the '*' sign.

In below program, we are trying to calculate the total penalty kicks taken by a team per week in practice. We have 3 variables that can help with this data. The integer variable **weeklypracticesessions** holds the number of team practice sessions per week, **playerstotal** is total number of players taking penalty kicks, and **penaltypicksperplayer** is the number of penalty kicks taken per player per session.

These 2 numbers are multiplied and stored in the variable **totalpenaltypicksperweek**, and this value is output on the screen.

```
1  weeklypracticesessions=2
2  playerstotal=15
3  penaltykicksperplayer=20
4  totalpenaltykicksperweek = weeklypracticesessions*playerstotal*penaltykicksperplayer
5
6  print("Total Team Penalty Kicks Per Week")
7  print(totalpenaltykicksperweek)
```

Output:

In the code, we multiply the 3 integer variables to get an output of **600** (2 x 15 x 20)

```
Total Team Penalty Kicks Per Week
600
```

Division and Remainder

Python does simple division using the '/' sign.

Python calculates remainder using the modulus or percentage '%' sign.

In the next program, we are given the total budget for a team this season and this is stored in the variable **totalseasonbudget**. We are only given the cost per game, and this is stored in the variable **costspergame**. We need to find the number of games that this team can afford, and the money left over after these games.

In line 4, we calculate the number of games that the team can afford. This is converted to an int variable (as the number of games cannot be a decimal). The value is stored in the integer variable **numberofgames**.

Money left over is calculated in line 5 as a remainder and is stored in integer value of **moneyleft**.

With a total season budget of 50000, and expenses of 8000 per game, the team can afford 6 games and 2000 is left over as seen in the output.

```
1    totalseasonbudget = 50000
2    costspergame = 8000
3
4    numberofgames = int(totalseasonbudget/costspergame)
5    moneyleft = totalseasonbudget%costspergame
6
7    print("No. of games team can afford to play")
8    print(numberofgames)
9    print("Money left at end of season")
10   print(moneyleft)
```

Output:

```
No. of games team can afford to play
6
Money left at end of season
2000
```

A Soccer Statistics Calculator

To demonstrate the concepts, we're going to create a program that calculates different basic statistics in soccer. The program takes in wins, losses, draws, goals scored and goals conceded by a team in a season. The program calculates total games played, total points, goal difference and average goals per game.

In lines 1-5, we declare integer variables **wins, losses, draws, goals_for** and **goals_against**. The user inputs integer values for each of them.

In line 7, variable **gamesplayed** calculates the sum of wins, losses and draws to get the number of games played.

In line 8, variable **points** stores the total number of points obtained by the team. 3 points for each win and 1 point for a draw.

In line 9, variable **goal_difference** is calculated as the difference between the goals scored and goals conceded.

In line 10, **goals_per_game** is the goals scored divided by total games played.

In lines 12-14, these statistics are printed using **fprint**.

```
1   wins = int(input("Enter the number of wins: "))
2   losses = int(input("Enter the number of losses: "))
3   draws= int(input("Enter the number of losses: "))
4   goals_for = int(input("Enter the number of goals scored this season: "))
5   goals_against = int(input("Enter the number of goals conceded this season: "))
6
7   gamesplayed=wins+losses+draws
8   points = wins*3+draws*1
9   goal_difference = goals_for - goals_against
10  goals_per_game = goals_for/gamesplayed
11
12  print(f"Total Points: {points} in {gamesplayed} games")
13  print(f"Goal Difference: {goal_difference}")
14  print(f"Average Goals Per Game: {goals_per_game} goals per game")
15
```

Output:

```
Enter the number of wins: 25
Enter the number of losses: 5
Enter the number of losses: 8
Enter the number of goals scored this season: 76
Enter the number of goals conceded this season: 65
Total Points: 83 in 38 games
Goal Difference: 11
Average Goals Per Game: 2.0 goals per game
```

Random numbers

In Python, we can generate random numbers and use it to create randomized output. In the code below, we use a random number to check if the goalkeeper dives the same side as the penalty taker shoots. We assume that the goalkeeper saves the goal if he dives to the correct side. This is done for 10 shots, and the number of goals scored is printed out at the end.

In line 1, we import Python library **random** which allows us to create and manipulate random variables.

In line 4-5, we declare **penalty_shots** and **goals** as variables for the total penalty shots taken and goals scored respectively. There are 10 penalty shots to be taken, and 0 goals initially.

In line 7, a for loop from 1 to 10(penalty_shots) is set up.

In line 8, a random variable **goalkeeper_side_dive** is set up. Random.random() is a function within the random library that creates a decimal number between 0 and 1. We multiply that by 2 to get a number between 0 and 2. If **goalkeeper_side_dive** is less than 1, then the goalkeeper dives the wrong way, and it is a goal. We increase the number of goals by 1.

If **goalkeeper_side_dive** is greater than 1, the goalkeeper dives the right way and saves the goal. After the loop ends, we print the number of goals scored.

```
import random

# Simulate a penalty shootout
penalty_shots = 10
goals = 0

for penalty in range(penalty_shots):
    goalkeeper_side_dive = random.random()*2

    if goalkeeper_side_dive < 1:
        print("The goalkeeper dived the wrong way. Goal!!")
        goals = goals + 1
    else:
        print("Saved! The goalkeeper made the right move. No Goal!!")

print(" ")
print("Total goals scored in 10 shots:", goals)
```

Output:

In below output, the goalkeeper dives the right way only 3 times. So, 7 goals out of 10 are scored. The result of the shot is seen after each of the 10 shots as either a goal or no goal. Run the program a couple of times to ensure that a different answer (random answer) is created each time.

```
The goalkeeper dived the wrong way. Goal!!
Saved! The goalkeeper made the right move. No Goal!!
The goalkeeper dived the wrong way. Goal!!
The goalkeeper dived the wrong way. Goal!!
Saved! The goalkeeper made the right move. No Goal!!
The goalkeeper dived the wrong way. Goal!!
The goalkeeper dived the wrong way. Goal!!
The goalkeeper dived the wrong way. Goal!!
Saved! The goalkeeper made the right move. No Goal!!
The goalkeeper dived the wrong way. Goal!!

Total goals scored in 10 shots: 7
```

Random Variable Example 2

In the next example, a team's manager wants to give a player a gift. He labels all 20 players in the squad 1-20 and puts the number into a hat. He pulls out a number randomly to pick the lucky winner. Now, let's do this with a Python program. In Line 1, we import the random library.

In line 2, we create the random variable **random_player** as a random number between 1 and 20. It is converted to integer to make sure that it is a whole number.

In line 5, the lucky player number is output on the screen.

```
1  import random
2  random_player = int(random.random()*20)
3
4  print(" ")
5  print("Lucky soccer player is Player Number ", random_player)
```

Output:

Run the program a few times to ensure that we get a different player every time.

```
Lucky soccer player is Player Number  5
```

```
Lucky soccer player is Player Number  16
```

```
Lucky soccer player is Player Number  4
```

The next few examples are great ways to show the use of Python as a calculator, but it requires knowledge of exponents, logarithms and square root which are normally only taught after year 8 in school. So, the rest of this chapter is great for kids over the age of 12.

Exponents

In the next problem, we have a soccer fan who just started a club last year. He's starting off with a very small base of 100 people, but he's confident that he can double his fan base every year. He's trying to figure out how many fans he'll have after 10 years.

```
1   new_club_fanbase = 100
2   growth_exp = 2
3   years = 10
4
5   fanbase_10years = new_club_fanbase * (growth_exp ** years)
6   print(f"After {years} years, the fanbase will be {fanbase_10years} fans.")
```

In line 1-3, we declare variables **new_club_fanbase, growth_exp** and **years** as for the current fan base number, growth rate and years to be taken into account for calculation respectively. **Growth_exp** is 2 since we expect the fanbase to double each year. Exponents are a great way to solve this. The formula is shown below:

$$fanbase\_10years = new\_club\_fanbase * (grwoth\_exp^{years})$$

In Python, we use the double star symbol for exponentiation (**) and the single star for multiplication (*).

This is shown in line 5 when the equation is written.

The output from the equation is printed on the screen in line 6.

Output:

As seen in the output, the club will have 102400 fans in 10 years.

`After 10 years, the fanbase will be 102400 fans.`

Logarithms

Logarithms are basically the reverse of exponents, and can be used to solve problems that are the inverse of the previous ones.

For example, what if the revenue of a club increases by 50% per year, and we want to figure out how many years it takes to get to $1 million. Logarithms are the best way to do so.

Logarithms are included in the math library in Python so we import the Math library in line 1.

The variables for initial revenue, target revenue and growth rate are declared in lines 3-5. A growth rate of 50% is indicated by a **growth_rate** of 0.5 below.

The formula to calculate number of years based on declared variables is:

$$years = \frac{\log \frac{target\_revenue}{initial\_revenue}}{\log(1 + growth\_rate)}$$

This is calculated in line 6 and converted into an integer variable (as we are looking for an approximate number of years).

```
import math

initial_revenue = 1000
target_revenue = 1000000
growth_rate = 0.5

years = int(math.log(target_revenue / initial_revenue) / math.log(1 + growth_rate))
print(f"It will take {years} years for the club to reach an annual revenue of $1 million.")
```

Output:

Based on the numbers and the formula, it takes this club 17 years to reach its goal.

```
It will take 17 years for the club to reach an annual revenue of $1 million.
```

Square root

Square roots in Python can be done using the **sqrt()** function in the Math library.

The problem we're trying to solve is that a soccer team has a square space of 2000 square meters to practice soccer. The team needs to calculate the length of each side, and that will help determine number of cones needed for each side of the square. Each cone covers 1 meter length of the side.

The math library in Python is used to calculate a lot of the basic and advanced math functionality.

So, it's good practice to import the Math library into Python when doing calculation. This is done in line 1 below.

In line 3, the variable **square_field** has an area of 2000.

In line 4, square root is calculated using **math.sqrt** of **square_field**. It is converted into int as we cannot have fractional cones to put on each side.

In line 6, we print out the number of cones needed.

```
1   import math
2
3   square_field = 2000;
4   length = int(math.sqrt(square_field))
5   number_cones = length;
6   print(f"It will take approximately {number_cones} cones per side to get a field of {square_field} square meters.")
```

Output:

Each side is 44 meters, which means 44 cones are needed for each side.

```
It will take approximately 44 cones per side to get a field of 2000 square meters.
```

Trigonometry

Basic trigonometry can be done in Python using the sin(), cos(), tan() functions in the Math library.

In the below program, the ball is 10 meters high, and at an angle of 30 degrees to the foot of the player. How far is the ball from the player's foot? To solve this problem, we use trigonometry.

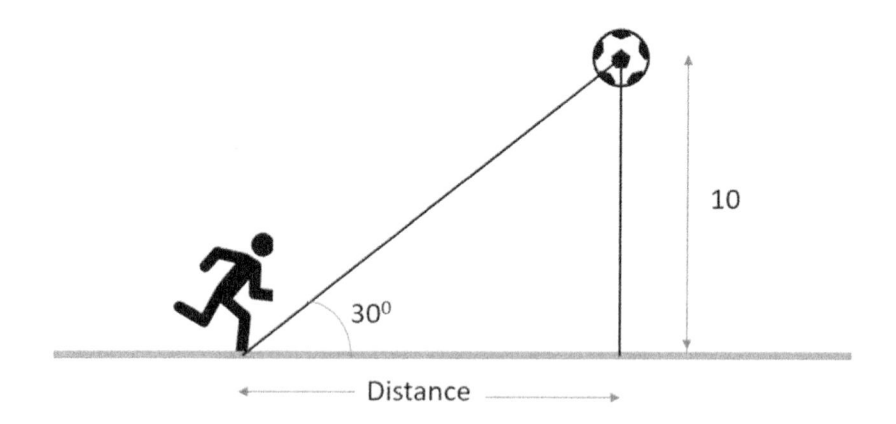

$$\tan(30) = \frac{10}{Distance}$$

$$Distance = \frac{10}{\tan(30)}$$

We use the tan function which is part of the Python math library. The functions work on angles in radian units.

The angle needs to be converted into radian using **math.radians** in line 3.

The distance is then calculated using the formula in line 5. The distance is a float variable with 10 decimal places. To make it more readable, we round it to two decimal places using the **round()** function in line 7.

The output is then printed on the screen in line 7.

```
1    import math
2    angle = 30
3    ang_rad=math.radians(angle)
4    v_dist = 10
5    h_dist=10/math.tan(ang_rad)
6    rounded_height=round(h_dist, 2)
7    print(f"The player is {rounded_height}m away from the player.")
```

Output:

```
The player is 17.32m away from the player
```

Exercises to practice
1. Create 10 variables to store the goals scored by a team in ten different games. Then calculate and print the total number of goals scored and average goals per game for those games.
2. Create a program that calculates the goal difference for a team given the goals scored and goals conceded which are stored in two different variables.
3. Calculate the average salary for a player per season given the salary per game and total number of games per season.
4. Create a Python program to determine how many players a soccer team can buy in the off season given its total player budget and the average cost per player. Use variables to store the total off season budget and the cost per player, and then calculate and print the number of players the team can afford, along with the money left over.
5. Pick a random player in a team of 11 to take a penalty shoot out and print out the player number on screen (eg. "Player 1 takes the shot", "Player 2 takes the shot" etc. etc.)
6. Create a Python program that simulates the growth of the Sydney League over the next 10 years, considering it has a fan base of 15000 and a growth rate of 20% per year. How many fans will it have after 10 years? Then, calculate how many years it will take to reach 1 million fans?

7. A square practice soccer field is 15 meters on each side. How much does it cost the team to water the field if it costs $100 per square meter to do so?

8. A soccer ball is 20 meters away from the goal and on the ground. The goal post bar is 10 meters high. What is the maximum angle a player can shoot at to ensure that it doesn't go over the bar?

Arrays in Python

An array is a group of variables of the same data type and with the same name. It helps with better organizing the code.

To demonstrate this, let's look at a simple example. If you want to store 10 numbers in 10 integer variables, we need to create 10 different integer variables as below.

num1=5

num2=6

num3=7

num4=9

num5=34

num6=9

num7=99

num8=67

num9=4

num10=3

With arrays, we can create the variable like this:

num = [5,6,7,9,34,9,99,67,4,3]

num is an array of size 10.

If we want to print the numbers, just print out the numbers using the index. The first index starts at 0. So, if we want to print out the first number, then:

print (num[0]) prints out 5.

print (num[1]) prints out 6 and so on.

Arrays use less computer memory and make programs run faster. They also help to organize code better and make code more understandable.

Now, let's look at an example where we input the names of 10 Premier League clubs into an array.

In line 1, we create an empty array called **soccer_clubs** that we can enter data into.

Lines 3-5 have a 10 item for-loop where we enter the names of the Premier League clubs.

In line 4, the user enters the name of the Premier League clubs and stores it in string **club_name**.

In line 5, **club_name** is added to array **soccer_clubs** using **append()** function. The **append** function is used to add items to the end of an array.

In line 8-9, we have another for loop that prints the items in the array.

```
1   soccer_clubs = []
2
3   for i in range(10):
4       club_name = input(f"Enter the name of soccer club {i + 1}: ")
5       soccer_clubs.append(club_name)
6
7   print("List of Premier League Soccer Clubs:")
8   for club in soccer_clubs:
9       print(club)
```

Output:

```
Enter the name of soccer club 1: Manchester United
Enter the name of soccer club 2: Manchester City
Enter the name of soccer club 3: Arsenal
Enter the name of soccer club 4: Tottenham Hotspurs
Enter the name of soccer club 5: Bolton Wanderers
Enter the name of soccer club 6: West Ham United
Enter the name of soccer club 7: Chelsea
Enter the name of soccer club 8: Liverpool
Enter the name of soccer club 9: Leicester City
Enter the name of soccer club 10: Ipswich City
List of Premier League Soccer Clubs:
Manchester United
Manchester City
Arsenal
Tottenham Hotspurs
Bolton Wanderers
West Ham United
Chelsea
Liverpool
Leicester City
Ipswich City
```

Adding and Removing Items from an Array

We can also add and remove elements in an array. To remove elements, we use the function remove() and to add elements we use the function **append()**.

In the number array at the start of the chapter, we can use **num.remove(67)** to remove the number 67 from the array. And we can add a new number (let's say 100) by using **num.append(100).**

In the next example, let's create an array of Premier League clubs and remove one club at the end of the season. And then, we add a newly promoted club to the array.

In line 1, we declare array **club_name** which contains names of 10 clubs in the premier league. In lines 4-5 we print the club names, so the user knows which clubs are there before any changes are made.

In line 6, the user inputs the club the user wants to remove, and it is stored in variable **relegatedclub**. In line 7, the user inputs the club the user wants to add and stores it in variable **promotedclub**.

And then, in lines 10-11, we print out all the list of club names with the new club.

```
club_name = ["Manchester United", "Manchester City", "Arsenal", "Tottenham Hotspur", "Bolton Wanderers", "West Ham United",
"Chelsea", "Liverpool", "Leicester City", "Ipswich City"]
print("The Premier League clubs are: ")
for club in club_name:
    print(club)
relegatedclub = input("Which club performed the worst last season?")
promotedclub = input("Which club was promoted last season?")
club_name.remove(relegatedclub)
club_name.append(promotedclub)
print("The new Premier League clubs are: ")
for club in club_name:
    print(club)
```

Output:

In this example, the **relegatedclub** is Chelsea and the **promotedclub** is Blackburn Rovers. This is the seen in the second list where Chelsea is remove and Blackburn Rovers is added.

```
The Premier League clubs are:
Manchester United
Manchester City
Arsenal
Tottenham Hotspur
Bolton Wanderers
West Ham United
Chelsea
Liverpool
Leicester City
Ipswich City
Which club performed the worst last season?Chelsea
Which club was promoted last season?Blackburn Robers
The new Premier League clubs are:
Manchester United
Manchester City
Arsenal
Tottenham Hotspur
Bolton Wanderers
West Ham United
Liverpool
Leicester City
Ipswich City
Blackburn Robers
```

Premier League teams with wins, losses and draws

We can also use elements in multiple arrays and create a third one that's a product of the two. For example, if num1 and num2 are two arrays such that:

num1 = [1,2,3]

num2 = [10,9,8]

Then we can create num3 which is a product of num1 and num2 using the zip function below:

num3 = [num1*num2 for num1, num2 in zip(num1,num2)]

zip is a function used to access data in multiple arrays at the same time. It can also be used in for loops.

Now, we get the result below:

num3 = [1*10,2*9,3*8]

num3 = [10, 18, 24]

In the next example, we create three arrays for the wins, losses and draws for three premier league teams. We then calculate the total points scored for each club and store it in a fourth array. Each team gets 3 points for a win and 1 for a draw.

In line 1, we declare array **club_name** which contains names of 10 clubs in the premier league. In lines 3-5, we create three arrays **club_wins, club_losses** and **club_draws** that contain the number of wins, losses and draws for the teams in array **club_name**.

In lines 7-8, we print the names of the clubs with the number of wins, losses and draws in a for loop. We need to use the zip function as it accesses data from multiple arrays.

In line 9, we use the zip function again to calculate the number of points for each team and store it in an array called **club_points**.

In line 12-13, we print out the names of the clubs with the number of points scored.

```
1   club_name = ["Manchester United", "Manchester City", "Arsenal", "Tottenham Hotspur", "Bolton Wanderers", "West Ham United",
2   "Chelsea", "Liverpool", "Leicester City", "Ipswich City"]
3   club_wins = [10,9,10,7,8,6,5,3,4,5]
4   club_losses = [4,3,5,3,2,2,2,4,2,1]
5   club_draws = [4,6,3,8,8,9,11,11,12,12]
6   print("The Premier League clubs are: ")
7   for club,wins,losses,draws in zip(club_name, club_wins, club_losses,club_draws):
8       print("Club " + club + " = "+ str(wins) + " Wins "+ str(losses) + " Losses " + str(draws) + " Draws ")
9   club_points = [club_wins*3+club_draws*1 for club_wins, club_draws in zip(club_wins, club_draws)]
10  print("")
11  print("Points")
12  for club,wins,losses, draws, points in zip(club_name, club_wins, club_losses,club_draws, club_points):
13      print("Club " + club + " = "+ str(points)+" Points")
14
```

Output:

```
The Premier League clubs are:
Club Manchester United= 10 Wins 4 Losses 4 Draws
Club Manchester City= 9 Wins 3 Losses 6 Draws
Club Arsenal= 10 Wins 5 Losses 3 Draws
Club Tottenham Hotspur= 7 Wins 3 Losses 8 Draws
Club Bolton Wanderers= 8 Wins 2 Losses 8 Draws
Club West Ham United= 6 Wins 2 Losses 9 Draws
Club Chelsea= 5 Wins 2 Losses 11 Draws
Club Liverpool= 3 Wins 4 Losses 11 Draws
Club Leicester City= 4 Wins 2 Losses 12 Draws
Club Ipswich City= 5 Wins 1 Losses 12 Draws

Points
Club Manchester United= 34 Points
Club Manchester City= 33 Points
Club Arsenal= 33 Points
Club Tottenham Hotspur= 29 Points
Club Bolton Wanderers= 32 Points
Club West Ham United= 27 Points
Club Chelsea= 26 Points
Club Liverpool= 20 Points
Club Leicester City= 24 Points
Club Ipswich City= 27 Points
```

Exercises to Practice

1. Create an array of 5 soccer players with another array containing number of goals scored by each player during the season. Print out the names of all players with the number of goals scored.
2. Create an array of 10 soccer teams with arrays containing the number of red cards and yellow cards each team had. Calculate a negative sportsmanship score. A higher score is worse. There are 10 points for each red card, and 3 points for a yellow. Print out the team names with their sportsmanship score.
3. Create an array of 8 soccer stadiums with arrays containing their capacity. Print out the values for each stadium.
4. Create an array of 6 soccer teams with arrays containing the number of goals scored and the number of goals conceded by each team in the current season. Calculate and print the goal difference (goals scored minus goals conceded) for each team.
5. Create an array of 10 soccer players with arrays containing the number of assists and the number of goals they've scored in the current season. Calculate and print the goal-to-assist ratio for each player.

Lists in Python

What is a List?

Another programming data structure that is very useful is a list. It also stores multiple elements like arrays, but it can store items of different data types. A single list can store both integer and string variables. For example, let's create a list below called **lista**.

lista = ['a','Tom',5,6.5,False]

lista contains 5 elements. 'a' and 'Tom' are string variables; 5 is an integer variable, 6.5 is a float variable and False is a Boolean.

A list is great for organizing data of different data types.

We can access different elements of a list using an index. The index of the first element is 0.

So, **print(lista[0])** prints 'a' on the screen.

print(lista[01]) prints 'Tom' on the screen.

We can add elements to a list using append function and remove elements from a list using the remove function.

lista.append(9) adds 9 to the end of the list. The list now becomes

lista = ['a','Tom',5, 6.5, False,9]

lista.remove(6.5) removes the first occurrence of 6.5 in lista. So, the list now becomes:

lista = ['a','Tom',5, False,9]

Lists with Multiple elements

If we create a list with multiple elements with the same data type, we need to create a reference to access the data.

In the example below, we want to create a list of 5 soccer players with player name, games played, and goals scored. So, we create a reference for each data value that is the same across the list. We create a reference "**name**" for all soccer names in the list; a reference "**games_played**" for games played and a reference "**goals_scored**" for number of goals scored. This is seen when creating the list **soccer_players** in lines 1-6.

When we access the data for printing, we use the reference name to access the data. In the for loop in line 10, player is a counter that iterates through **soccer_players**. We use **player['name']** to access name data, **player['games_played']** to access games played data, and **player['goals_scored']** to access goals scored data. This is seen when printing the output below.

```python
soccer_players = [
    {"name": "Lionel Messi", "games_played": 800, "goals_scored": 700},
    {"name": "Cristiano Ronaldo", "games_played": 850, "goals_scored": 750},
    {"name": "Neymar Jr.", "games_played": 600, "goals_scored": 300},
    {"name": "Kylian Mbappé", "games_played": 250, "goals_scored": 150},
    {"name": "Robert Lewandowski", "games_played": 400, "goals_scored": 380},
]

print("List of Soccer Players:")
for player in soccer_players:
    print(f"Name: {player['name']}")
    print(f"Games Played: {player['games_played']}")
    print(f"Goals Scored: {player['goals_scored']}")
    print()
```

Output:

```
List of Soccer Players:
Name: Lionel Messi
Games Played: 800
Goals Scored: 700

Name: Cristiano Ronaldo
Games Played: 850
Goals Scored: 750

Name: Neymar Jr.
Games Played: 600
Goals Scored: 300

Name: Kylian Mbappé
Games Played: 250
Goals Scored: 150

Name: Robert Lewandowski
Games Played: 400
Goals Scored: 380
```

Sorting data in a list

To sort data in a list, we use a function called **sorted()**. If there are multiple elements in a list, we can sort based on one of the elements of the list. In the above example, we can sort the players based on the number of goals scored. They can be sorted in ascending or descending order. In this case, we will sort it in descending order.

To sort the data, we add line 9 in program below. We create a new list called **sorted_players** which contains the list sorted in descending order of goals scored.

Here's the elements of the sorted() function with their explanations:

soccer_players is the list of players we want to sort that is an input into sorted()

key = lambda x: x["goals scored"] :This is a key function that tells sorted() how to extract the sorting key from each element in **soccer_players**. In this case, it's a lambda function that takes an element x and returns the element with a reference name of goals scored. This means you are sorting the elements in **club_info** based on the values in **goals_scored** in the list.

reverse=True means that you are sorting in descending order of value. reverse=False would sort in ascending order of value.

In the output below, we see that the list is now sorted with the highest goal scorer at the top of the list, and the lowest at the bottom.

```python
soccer_players = [
    {"name": "Lionel Messi", "games_played": 800, "goals_scored": 700},
    {"name": "Cristiano Ronaldo", "games_played": 850, "goals_scored": 750},
    {"name": "Neymar Jr.", "games_played": 600, "goals_scored": 300},
    {"name": "Kylian Mbappé", "games_played": 250, "goals_scored": 150},
    {"name": "Robert Lewandowski", "games_played": 400, "goals_scored": 380},
]

sorted_players = sorted(soccer_players, key=lambda x: x["goals_scored"], reverse=True)

print("Soccer Players Sorted by Goals Scored:")
for player in sorted_players:
    print(f"Name: {player['name']}")
    print(f"Games Played: {player['games_played']}")
    print(f"Goals Scored: {player['goals_scored']}")
    print()
```

Output:

```
Soccer Players Sorted by Goals Scored:
Name: Cristiano Ronaldo
Games Played: 850
Goals Scored: 750

Name: Lionel Messi
Games Played: 800
Goals Scored: 700

Name: Robert Lewandowski
Games Played: 400
Goals Scored: 380

Name: Neymar Jr.
Games Played: 600
Goals Scored: 300

Name: Kylian Mbappé
Games Played: 250
Goals Scored: 150
```

Now, we do the same sorting operation for the Premier league table created in the previous chapter on arrays.

We create a list **club_info** of club names and points scored in line 8.

We then use the **sorted()** function in line 10 to create a sorted array called **sorted_clubs**. It sorts **club_info** in descending order based on the values in **club_points**. **x[1]** indicates that the sorting is done based on the 2nd element of the list(which is **club_points**). So, this means that the Premier league clubs are being sorted based on total number of points in descending order.

```
club_name = ["Manchester United", "Manchester City", "Arsenal", "Tottenham Hotspur", "Bolton Wanderers", "West Ham United",
             "Chelsea", "Liverpool", "Leicester City", "Ipswich City"]
club_wins = [10, 9, 10, 7, 8, 6, 5, 3, 4, 5]
club_losses = [4, 3, 5, 3, 1, 2, 2, 4, 2, 1]
club_draws = [4, 6, 3, 8, 8, 9, 11, 11, 12, 10]
club_points = [club_wins * 3 + club_draws * 1 for club_wins, club_draws in zip(club_wins, club_draws)]

club_info = list(zip(club_name, club_points))

sorted_clubs = sorted(club_info, key=lambda x: x[1], reverse=True)

print("Premier League clubs sorted by points (descending order):")
for club, points in sorted_clubs:
    print(f"Club {club} = {points} Points")
```

```
Premier League clubs sorted by points (descending order):
Club Manchester United = 34 Points
Club Manchester City = 33 Points
Club Arsenal = 33 Points
Club Bolton Wanderers = 32 Points
Club Tottenham Hotspur = 29 Points
Club West Ham United = 27 Points
Club Ipswich City = 27 Points
Club Chelsea = 26 Points
Club Leicester City = 24 Points
Club Liverpool = 20 Points
```

Accessing and Modifying elements in a list

We already know we can access elements of a list using an index value. We can also figure where an element occurs in the list using a function called index.

In the below example, we modify the Premier league table based on the results of a match. We add 3 points to the winner's total; or 1 point to both teams playing if it's a draw.

In lines 8-9, we accept user input for names of teams playing, and store the team names in variables **team1** and **team2**.

In line 11, we accept the result of the match. The user inputs 1 for team1 win, 2 for team2 win and 3 for a draw.

The value is stored in a integer variable called **result**.

We then use the index function to figure out where in the list each team is located.

team1_index is an integer variable that stores the list index value of team1. It basically searches through the list for occurrence of team1 value and stores it. If the value does not occur, it stores a value of -1.

team2_index does the same for the index value of team2.

Based on the index value, the result value is added to **team2_index**.

If result is 1, the value of **club_points** at **team1index** are increased by 3; meaning that team 1 gets 3 points added. (line 16-17)

If result is 2, the value of **club_points** at **team2index** are increased by 3; meaning that team 2 gets 3 points added. (line 18-19)

If result is 3, the value of **club_points** at both **team1index** and **team2index** are increased by 1; meaning that both team 1 and team 2 gets 1 point added. (line 20-22).

The clubs are then sorted based on points; and the Premier League points table is printed out.

This is shown in output below the code.

```python
club_name = ["Manchester United", "Manchester City", "Arsenal", "Tottenham Hotspur", "Bolton Wanderers", "West Ham United",
             "Chelsea", "Liverpool", "Leicester City", "Ipswich City"]
club_wins = [10, 9, 10, 7, 8, 6, 5, 3, 4, 5]
club_losses = [4, 3, 5, 3, 2, 2, 2, 4, 2, 1]
club_draws = [4, 6, 3, 8, 8, 9, 11, 11, 12, 13]
club_points = [club_wins * 3 + club_draws * 1 for club_wins, club_draws in zip(club_wins, club_draws)]

team1 = input("Enter the name of the home team: ")
team2 = input("Enter the name of the away team: ")

result = input("Enter the result of the match (1 for home team win, 2 for away team win, 0 for a draw): ")

team1_index = club_name.index(team1)
team2_index = club_name.index(team2)

if result == "1":
    club_points[team1_index] += 3
elif result == "2":
    club_points[team2_index] += 3
elif result == "0":
    club_points[team1_index] += 1
    club_points[team2_index] += 1

print("\nUpdated Premier League clubs sorted by points (descending order):")
club_info = list(zip(club_name, club_points))

sorted_clubs = sorted(club_info, key=lambda x: x[1], reverse=True)
for club, points in sorted_clubs:
    print(f"Club {club} = {points} Points")
```

Output:

```
Enter the name of the home team: Manchester United
Enter the name of the away team: Arsenal
Enter the result of the match (1 for home team win, 2 for away team win, 0 for a draw): 0

Updated Premier League clubs sorted by points (descending order):
Club Manchester United = 35 Points
Club Arsenal = 34 Points
Club Manchester City = 33 Points
Club Bolton Wanderers = 32 Points
Club Tottenham Hotspur = 29 Points
Club West Ham United = 27 Points
Club Ipswich City = 27 Points
Club Chelsea = 26 Points
Club Leicester City = 24 Points
Club Liverpool = 20 Points
```

Exercises to Practice

1. Create a list of 10 soccer stadiums with stadium name, stadium city and stadium capacity. Sort the stadiums based on stadium capacity and print them out.
2. Create a list of 5 soccer players with player name, champions league medals won, world cup medals won; and sort them based on total medals won.
3. Create a list of 10 soccer clubs with club name, club city, and the year the club was founded. Sort the clubs based on the founding year in ascending order and print them out.
4. Create a list of 8 national soccer teams with team name, FIFA World Rankings, and the number of World Cup titles won. Sort the national teams based on their FIFA World Rankings in ascending order and print them out.

Drawing in Python

Now, let's get to the really fun part. Drawing, Art, Animation, whatever you like to call it. Python can do it too. Drawing soccer objects and images is a great way to learn Python.

In Python, we're going to draw using the turtle library. The turtle library is a graphics library. It lets user draw on the screen as if one were using a pen. We invoke the use of the turtle library using the line:

import turtle

The turtle library has several functions that one can use to draw objects such as lines, squares, rectangles, circles etc.

We're going to learn these functions through the use of 5 examples in this chapter. First, we're going to learn how to draw a line. Using that knowledge, we're going to learn how to draw a rectangle. Then we're going to draw a circle. Using the knowledge from drawings we just completed, we're going to now draw a green soccer field with all the relevant lines in it. And then add a soccer ball to the center of the field.

Before we get started, let's go over the different steps involved in drawing something:

1. Create a screen object. This causes turtle to open a new screen.
2. Create a turtle object that can be used as a pen.
3. Assign a pen speed. This is the speed that the program would draw at.
4. Determine the coordinates of the item you want to draw.
5. Figure out the starting point. This is where the pen starts.
6. Determine the pen color. This is the color that the object is drawn in, and the color the shape is filled in with.

Now, let's get started.

Drawing a Line

In the program below, we're going to draw three lines of 3 different colors and 3 different thicknesses at 3 different locations on the screen.

In line 1, we import the **turtle** library so we can use the drawing functions.

In line 3, we create a screen object, to draw items on it.

In line 5, we create a turtle object called **pen**. This object will be used to draw on the screen object. Think of it as holding a pen and drawing on a screen.

In line 7, we set the speed for the object. A faster speed is good for drawing larger items, while a slower speed works for small items like lines, circles etc. We recommend a smaller speed while doing your first programs.

Lines 9-14: The first line is created. It is a red line with size 2.

In line 10, we start the drawing at (-150,0) which is the location on the screen. In line 11, we use the **pendown()** function to start drawing. Think of it as putting the pen down on a blank piece of paper. After **pendown()** function is invoked, all marks will be seen on the screen. In line 12, we set the pen size as 2 using the **pensize()** function. In line 13, we set the color as red using the **pencolor()** function. In line 14, we create a line of 200 pixels moving the pen to the right using the **forward()** function. The default direction for the forward function is to the right. We can change the default direction if we need to by using the rotate() function.

In lines 16-21, we create a line of size 4 that is blue in color. It is double in thickness of the first line and starts at (0,-50). The starting point is 150 pixels higher than the first line, and 50 pixels to the right.

In lines 23-28, we create the final line of size 6 that is green in color. It is three times the thickness of the first line and starts at (100,50). The starting point is 200 pixels higher than the first line and 100 pixels to the right.

Finally, in line 30, the programs stops with a **screen.exitonclick()** function. When this function is called, the screen closes when the user anywhere on the screen.

All three lines are seen in the output below the code.

```
1    import turtle
2
3    screen = turtle.Screen()
4
5    pen = turtle.Turtle()
6
7    pen.speed(1)
8
9    pen.penup()
10   pen.goto(-150, 0)
11   pen.pendown()
12   pen.pensize(2)
13   pen.pencolor("red")
14   pen.forward(200)
15
16   pen.penup()
17   pen.goto(0, -50)
18   pen.pendown()
19   pen.pensize(4)
20   pen.pencolor("blue")
21   pen.forward(150)
22
23   pen.penup()
24   pen.goto(100, 50)
25   pen.pendown()
26   pen.pensize(6)
27   pen.pencolor("green")
28   pen.forward(100)
29
30   screen.exitonclick()
```

Output:

Drawing a Rectangle

In the next example, we create a rectangle in Python by drawing 4 red lines. Then we fill the rectangle with red color.

In lines 1-7, we create the screen and pen objects and set the speed as in the previous program.

In line 9, we set a **begin_fill()** function as it is required to start filling of an object in turtle. We set the color as red in line 10.

In line 12-14, we start the program by getting the pen to coordinates **(-350,-300)** which is the bottom left of the screen.

In line 16, we draw a line of length 600 by moving the pen to the right with the **forward()** function. This draws the first line of the rectangle.

For the second line, we need to move up instead of right. We must change the direction the **forward()** function moves by rotating the direction.

In line 17, we rotate the pen to the left by 90 degrees using the function **left(90)**. Then, in line 18, we move the pen up a length of 200. In line 19, we rotate the pen to the left another 90 degrees for the third line of the rectangle.

In line 20-23, we repeat above steps by drawing a line of length 600 to the left, rotating 90 degrees. And we finally complete the rectangle by drawing a length of length 200 down.

In line 25, we fill the rectangle with **end_fill()** function.

The red rectangle is seen in the output below the code.

```
1   import turtle
2
3   screen = turtle.Screen()
4
5   pen = turtle.Turtle()
6
7   pen.speed(1)
8
9   pen.begin_fill()
10  pen.fillcolor("red")
11
12  pen.penup()
13  pen.goto(-350, -300)
14  pen.pendown()
15
16  pen.forward(600)
17  pen.left(90)
18  pen.forward(200)
19  pen.left(90)
20  pen.forward(600)
21  pen.left(90)
22  pen.forward(200)
23  pen.left(90)
24
25  pen.end_fill()
26  screen.exitonclick()
27
28
```

Output:

Drawing a Circle

In the next example, we draw a blue circle with a diameter of 200. It is done using the **circle(200)** function in line 16.

In lines 1-10, the process is similar to the previous problems where a screen object and pen object are created. The speed is set to 1, and the color is set to blue.

We start the drawing at (-100,-100) using the **goto(-100,-100)** function. These are the coordinates of the bottom of the circle (and not the center).

In line 18, we use the **end_fill()** to complete filling the circle.

We see the blue circle on the screen in the output below the code.

```
1   import turtle
2
3   screen = turtle.Screen()
4
5   pen = turtle.Turtle()
6
7   pen.speed(1)
8
9   pen.begin_fill()
10  pen.fillcolor("blue")
11
12  pen.penup()
13  pen.goto(-100, -100)
14  pen.pendown()
15
16  pen.circle(200)
17
18  pen.end_fill()
19
20  screen.exitonclick()
```

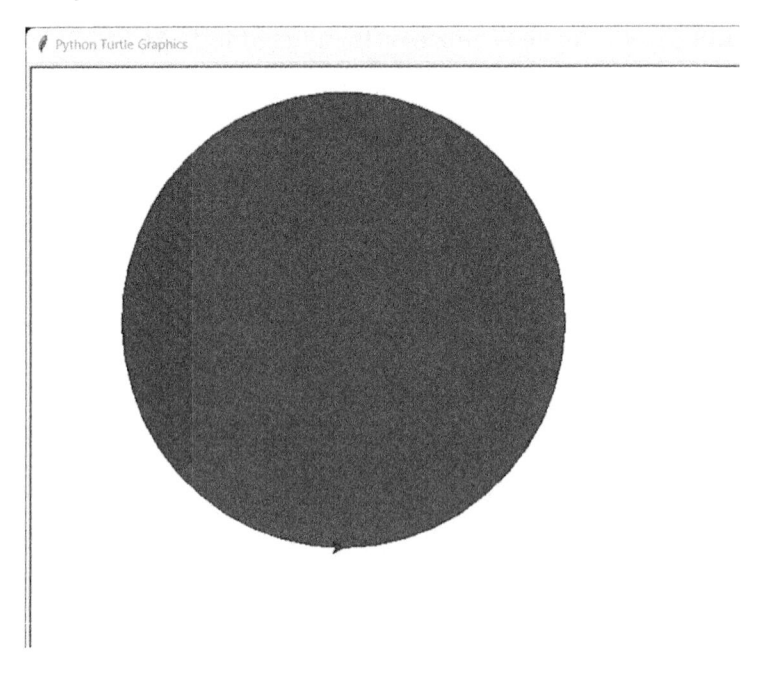

Output:

Drawing a Soccer Field

Now for the soccer part. Let's use the knowledge we have from the previous drawings and draw a full soccer field. That's right!!

We're going to draw a green rectangle which represents the soccer field grass. Then we're going to draw a line that goes through the center of the screen. This is the halfway line.

In the next step, we draw the center circle in the center of the field.

Then, we draw the left penalty box which is a white rectangle at the left-hand corner of the field. We do the same for the right penalty box which is on the right-hand corner of the field.

Finally, we draw a white spot at the center of the field, which is the kick off spot.

So, let's start off with the field.

Drawing the Green Rectangle (Lines 9-21)

The rectangle starts from the bottom left of the screen at (-300, -200) and is set up for a length of 600 and width of 400. It is filled with green which simulates the grass in the soccer field.

Drawing the Center Line (Lines 23-29)

The center line is drawn from the bottom center of the rectangle at (0,-200). The pensize is increased to 4 to increase visibility, and it set to color white.

Since the last direction for the forward() function in the program was to move down (last line in the rectangle), we need to add an extra 180 degree rotation in line 28 to make it move up. After the rotation, it moves up for a distance of 400, so that the center line width of the field.

Drawing the Center Circle (Lines 32-35)

The center circle is set to a width of 50. So, it starts at (50,0) which is the bottom of the circle.

Left Penalty Area (Lines 37-47)

The left penalty area is a rectangle in white. We start at the top left corner and start moving right. However, in the last line, we moved up while drawing the center line. So, we rotate the pen to the right by 90 degrees in line 40. The rectangle has a width of 50 and a length of 100.

Right Penalty Area (Lines 49-59)

Now, we do the same for the right-hand side. We start at the top right corner and create a rectangle again with a width of 50 and length of 100.

Center Dot (Lines 61-64)

Finally, we create a dot at the center of the center circle. This is the kickoff spot. It is set to a thickness of 10 and a location of (0,0).

We see the green soccer field drawn below the output code.

```
1   import turtle
2
3   screen = turtle.Screen()
4
5   pen = turtle.Turtle()
6
7   pen.speed(2)
8
9   pen.penup()
10  pen.goto(-300, -200)
11  pen.pendown()
12  pen.begin_fill()
13  pen.fillcolor("green")
14  pen.forward(600)
15  pen.left(90)
16  pen.forward(400)
17  pen.left(90)
18  pen.forward(600)
19  pen.left(90)
20  pen.forward(400)
21  pen.end_fill()
22
23  pen.penup()
24  pen.goto(0, -200)
25  pen.pendown()
26  pen.pensize(4)
27  pen.pencolor("white")
28  pen.left(180)
29  pen.forward(400)
30
31
```

```
32    pen.penup()
33    pen.goto(50, 0)
34    pen.pendown()
35    pen.circle(50)
36
37    pen.penup()
38    pen.goto(-300, 50)
39    pen.pendown()
40    pen.right(90)
41    pen.forward(50)
42    pen.right(90)
43    pen.forward(100)
44    pen.right(90)
45    pen.forward(100)
46    pen.right(90)
47    pen.forward(50)
48
49    pen.penup()
50    pen.goto(300, 50)
51    pen.pendown()
52    pen.left(90)
53    pen.forward(50)
54    pen.left(90)
55    pen.forward(100)
56    pen.left(90)
57    pen.forward(50)
58    pen.left(90)
59    pen.forward(100)
60
61    pen.penup()
62    pen.goto(0, 0)
63    pen.pendown()
64    pen.dot(10)
65
66    screen.exitonclick()
```

Output:

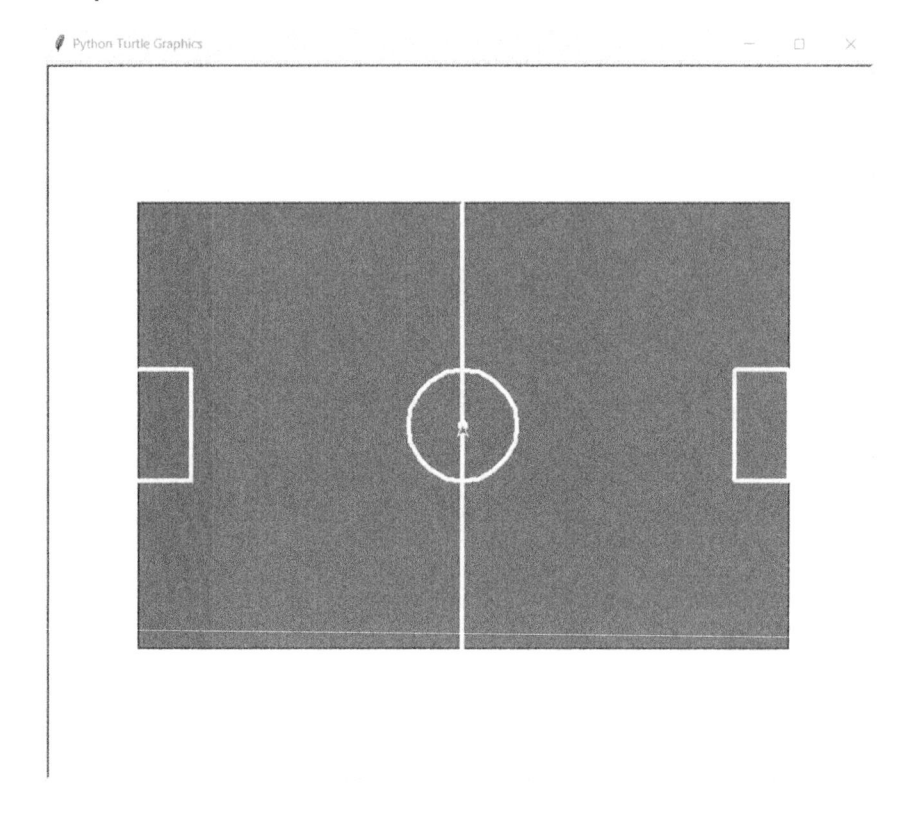

Drawing a Soccer Ball on a Soccer Field

In this example, we take the soccer field from the previous program and draw a black soccer ball in the middle of the field. So, we basically use the same program as in the previous example and add lines 66-73 to the program. The soccer ball is a circle of size 5 and filled with black color. In line 69, the color of the circle outline is set as black. And, in line 71, the color of the circle interior is set to black as well. This needs to be done as the interior of the ball needs to be filled.

In line 67, the pen is set to start at bottom corner of the circle at (5,0). And in line 72, the circle is drawn with a radius set as a size 5.

```python
import turtle

screen = turtle.Screen()

pen = turtle.Turtle()

pen.speed(2)

pen.penup()
pen.goto(-300, -200)
pen.pendown()
pen.begin_fill()
pen.fillcolor("green")
pen.forward(600)
pen.left(90)
pen.forward(400)
pen.left(90)
pen.forward(600)
pen.left(90)
pen.forward(400)
pen.end_fill()

pen.penup()
pen.goto(0, -200)
pen.pendown()
pen.pensize(4)
pen.pencolor("white")
pen.left(180)
pen.forward(400)


```

```
32      pen.penup()
33      pen.goto(50, 0)
34      pen.pendown()
35      pen.circle(50)
36
37      pen.penup()
38      pen.goto(-300, 50)
39      pen.pendown()
40      pen.right(90)
41      pen.forward(50)
42      pen.right(90)
43      pen.forward(100)
44      pen.right(90)
45      pen.forward(100)
46      pen.right(90)
47      pen.forward(50)
48
49      pen.penup()
50      pen.goto(300, 50)
51      pen.pendown()
52      pen.left(90)
53      pen.forward(50)
54      pen.left(90)
55      pen.forward(100)
56      pen.left(90)
57      pen.forward(50)
58      pen.left(90)
59      pen.forward(100)
60
61      pen.penup()
62      pen.goto(0, 0)
63      pen.pendown()
64      pen.dot(10)
```

```
66    pen.penup()
67    pen.goto(5, 0)
68    pen.begin_fill()
69    pen.pencolor("black")
70    pen.pendown()
71    pen.fillcolor("black")
72    pen.circle(5)
73    pen.end_fill()
74
75    screen.exitonclick()
```

Output:

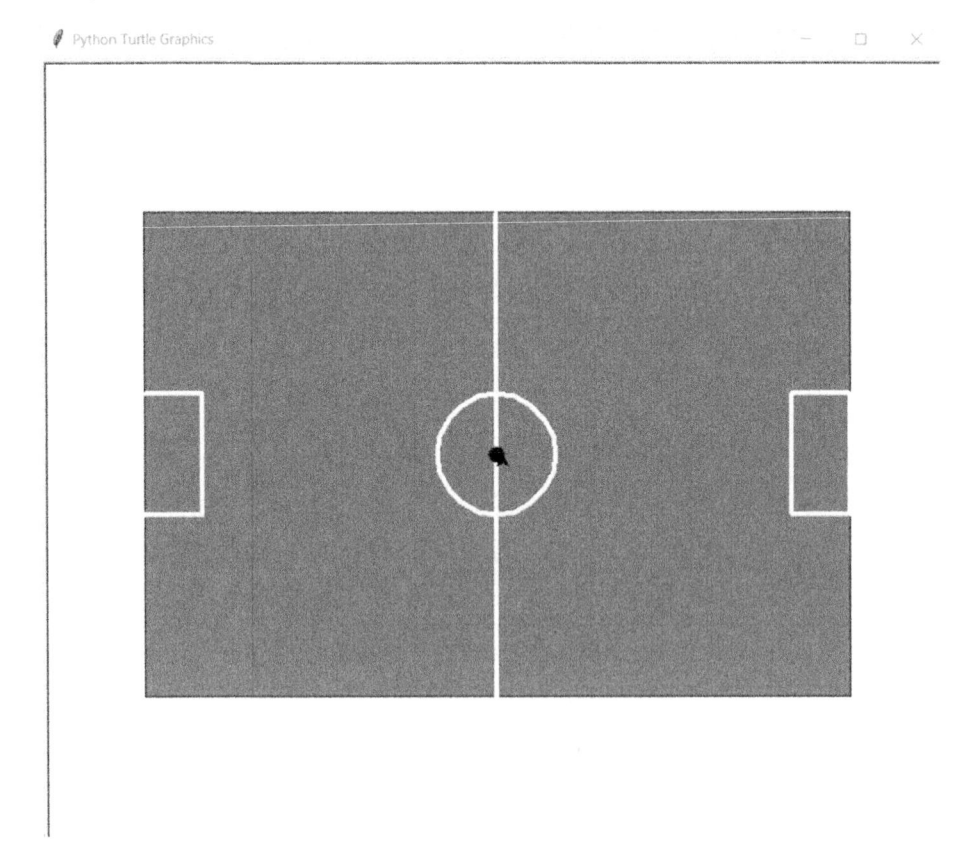

Exercises to Practice

1. Draw the following lines on a Python screen:
    a. A purple horizontal line of a certain thickness at the bottom left of the screen.
    b. A green vertical line of double the thickness of the previous line, in the center of the screen.
    c. A red vertical line of double the thickness of the previous line anywhere on the screen.
2. Draw a rectangle filled with green and fit 4 soccer balls on the 4 corners of the screen which have 4 different colors.
3. Draw a soccer ball with a cross in the middle. The cross is basically two diametric lines at 90 degrees to each other.
4. Draw a square green practice soccer field. This soccer field has:
    a. 4 orange dots at the 4 corners, which represent 4 soccer cones.
    b. One black circle in the center which represents a dummy.
    c. 2 blue soccer balls near the ends of the soccer cones. You can pick any two soccer cones.

    This simulates a practice session where players try to pass the ball to each other trying to avoid the dummy in the middle.

Moving a Soccer Ball on the Screen

Now, let's have some more fun.

We can actually move items on the turtle screen. We're going to create a soccer field and a ball that can move on the soccer field. The ball moves in the direction that the user presses the arrow keys on the keyboard.

The first step we do is to create a screen. Then, we create a vertical line that goes through the center of the screen. This is the center line that cuts the soccer field in half.

Then, we create a circle at the center of the screen which is the center circle of the field.

Next, we create a black soccer ball which starts at the center of the field.

For the soccer ball, we create functions that move the soccer ball up, down, right and left. These functions determine how far the soccer ball coordinates move each time we want it to move in that direction.

And finally, we determine which of the above functions are activated when certain keys on the keyboard are pressed. For example, if the right direction key on the keyboard is pressed, we'd ask the program to run the function that moves the soccer ball to the right.

Now that we have an outline, let's look at the actual program below.

In Lines 1-5 of the program, we create a turtle screen object and set it to a green color.

Then, in lines 7-12, we create the center line. The center line is created as the center of the entire screen. So, it doesn't matter if we change the screen size. The line will always be in the center. (Remember, in the last program, we made the line the center of a green rectangle). To do so, we create a turtle object called **line**. The line is set to **white** color and is set to go from (0, **-screen.window_height**/2) to (0, **screen.window_height**/2). **Screen.window_height** is the vertical height of the window. This makes the center line stretch to the size of the window while remaining in the center.

In lines 14-19, we create the center circle of the field to a radius of 100. A turtle object called **midcircle** is created to achieve this. This is done in exactly the same way as the previous program. It is set to **white** color and starts at **(0,-100)** which is the bottom of the circle.

```
1   import turtle
2
3   screen = turtle.Screen()
4   screen.title("Moving Circle with Center Line")
5   screen.bgcolor("green")
6
7   line = turtle.Turtle()
8   line.penup()
9   line.color("white")
10  line.goto(0, -screen.window_height() // 2)
11  line.pendown()
12  line.goto(0, screen.window_height() // 2)
13
14  midcircle = turtle.Turtle()
15  midcircle.penup()
16  midcircle.color("white")
17  midcircle.goto(0, -100)
18  midcircle.pendown()
19  midcircle.circle(100)
```

In lines 21-27, we create the drawing of the soccer ball. We create an object called **soccerball** which is right at the center of the screen and is filled with black color.

In lines 29-46, we create the functions that move the ball in the direction we want. The code in lines 29-30 create the function **moveto(x,y)** that move the ball to location with x-coordinate x and y-coordinate y.

We create the functions **move_left()**, **move_right()**, **move_up()** and **move_down()** which move the soccer ball left, right, up and down respectively.

To explain how these functions work, let's look at one of these functions **move_left()**. In **move_left()** in line 32, we set the values x and y as the current x and y co-ordinates of the **soccerball** object. Then, in line 33, we subtract the x value by 20. This simulates the motion of the ball to the left by 20. If we want the ball to move faster, we increase this from 20 to 30/40/50 etc. If we want the ball to move slower, we reduce the value. And then, in line 34, we call the function **move_to(x,y)** with the new values of x and y. This moves the soccer ball to the new x and y locations.

The function **move_right()** similarly adds 20 to x, the **soccerball** right by 20. The function **move_up()** adds 20 to y, and moves **soccerball** up. The function **move_down()** reduces y by 20 to move **soccerball** down by 20.

In lines 48-53, we check if the user clicks on the arrow buttons. For example, in line 48, the program checks if the user has clicked on the **"Left"** button. If this has happened, then it runs the function **move_left()** and the ball moves left. The same check is done for the user clicking the **"Right", "Up"** and **"Down"** button.

The **screen.listen()** function in line 52 makes sure that the screen is checking if the user touches keys on the keyboard.

The **screen.mailoop()** function in line 53 makes sure that the program keeps running after the user has typed in one of the buttons.

```python
soccerball = turtle.Turtle()
soccerball.shape("circle")
soccerball.color("black")
soccerball.penup()
soccerball.speed(1)

soccerball.goto(0, 0)

def move_to(x, y):
    soccerball.goto(x, y)
def move_left():
    x, y = soccerball.xcor(), soccerball.ycor()
    x -= 20
    move_to(x, y)
def move_right():
    x, y = soccerball.xcor(), soccerball.ycor()
    x += 20
    move_to(x, y)
def move_up():
    x, y = soccerball.xcor(), soccerball.ycor()
    y += 20
    move_to(x, y)
def move_down():
    x, y = soccerball.xcor(), soccerball.ycor()
    y -= 20
    move_to(x, y)

screen.onkey(move_left, "Left")
screen.onkey(move_right, "Right")
screen.onkey(move_up, "Up")
screen.onkey(move_down, "Down")
screen.listen()
screen.mainloop()
```

Output:

At Start:

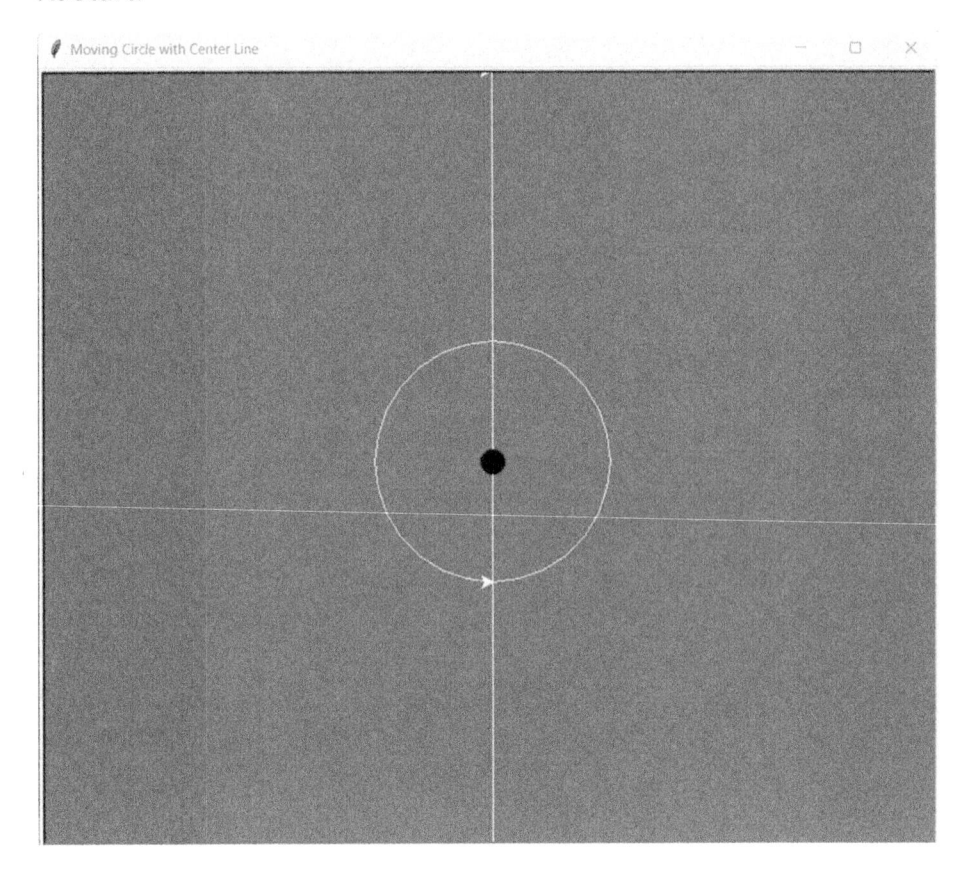

After Moving Ball Right Twice (Right by 40):

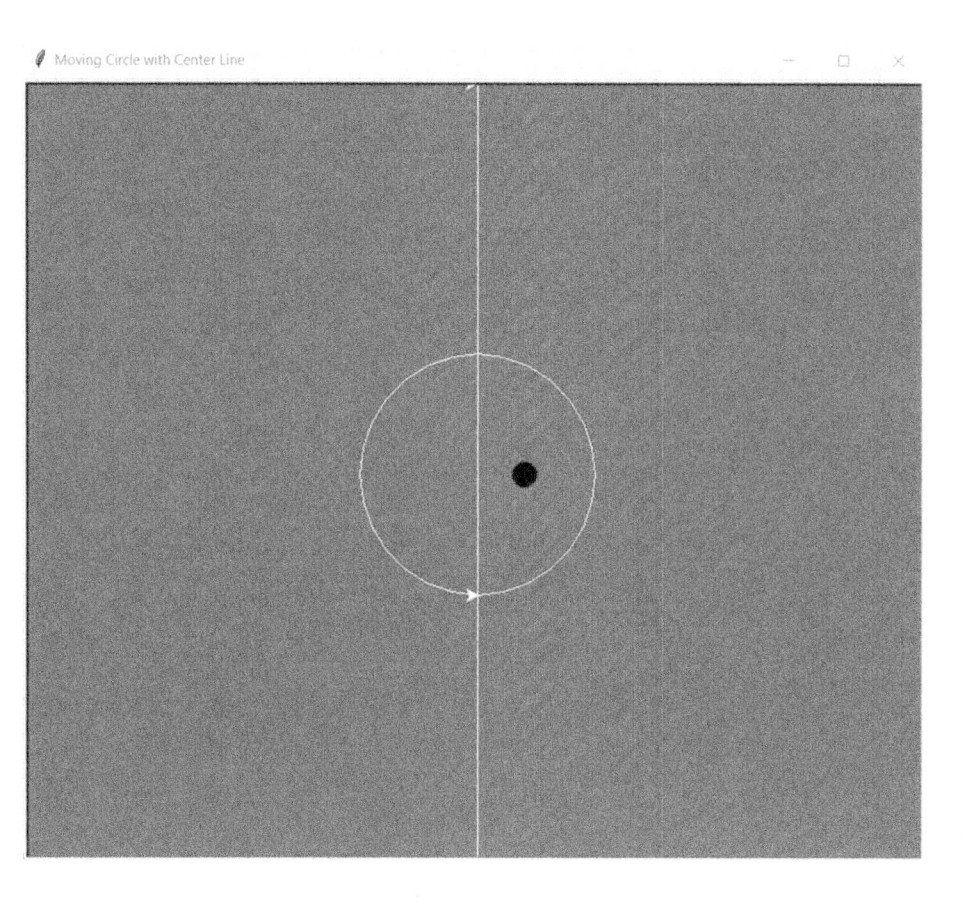

Moving Ball Down Four Times (Down by 80):

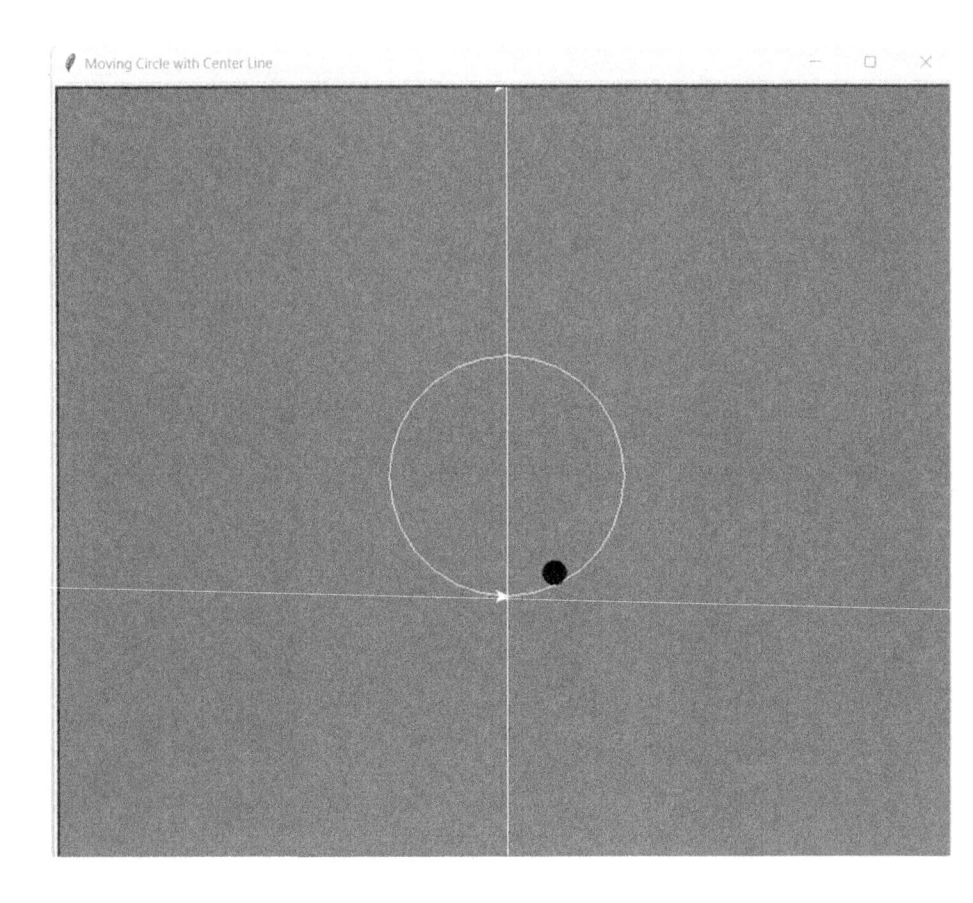

Moving Ball Left Six Times (Left by 120):

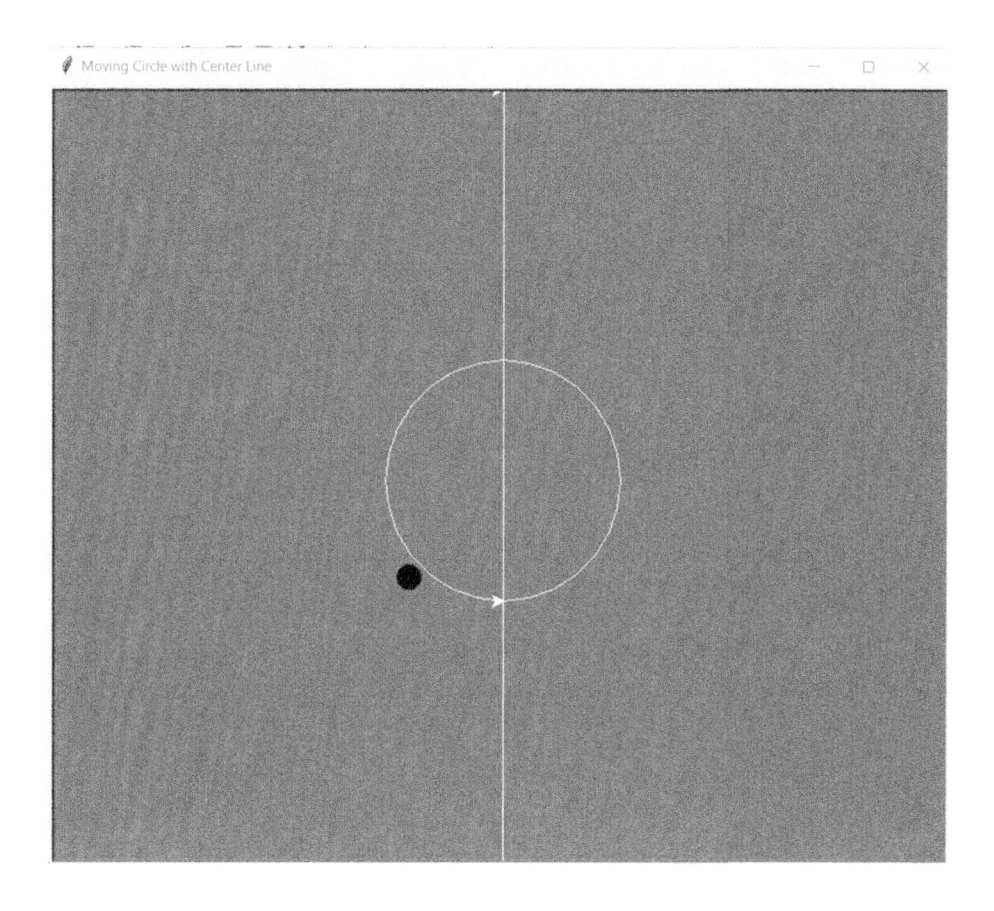

Moving Ball Up Twice (Up by 40):

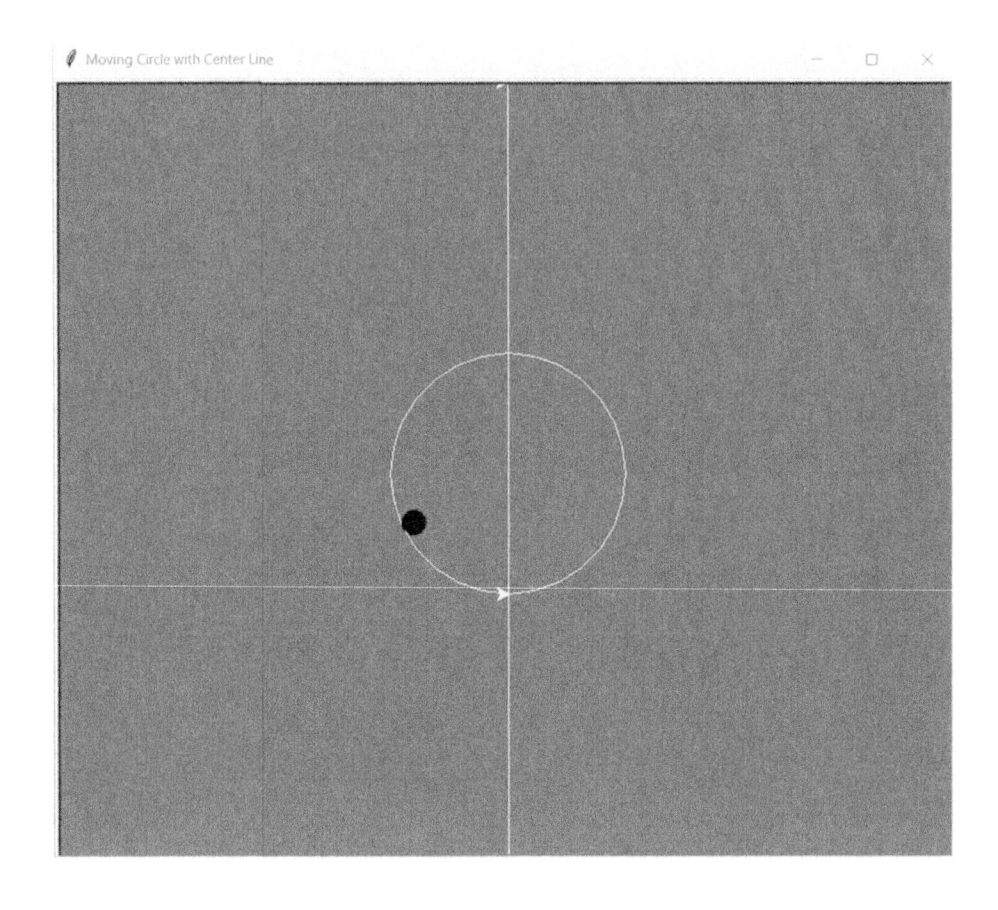

Exercises to Practice

1. Using the same code for soccer field above:
    a. Add two rectangles to the right and left that simulate soccer goal position.
    b. Check if the ball has reached the right goal. Increase the number of goals by 1 for team 1 if that happens, and restart location to center.
    c. Check if the ball has reached the left goal. Increase the number of goals by 1 for team 2 if that happens, and restart location to center.
    d. Double the speed of motion of the ball and see what happens.

Practice Test

All right. We've reached the end of the theory section of the book. It's time to test your skills. We have a 25 question quiz now so you have the chance to apply all that you've learnt so far.

Question 1

Why is Python a great language to start programming with?

    a. It is a simple and easy to read open-source language, with a large community.

    b. It is the most powerful computing language.

    c. It has the best graphics.

    d. It is the best for programming websites.

Question 2

Which website do you download python from?

    a. www.facebook.com

    b. www.youtube.com

    c. www.python.org/downloads/

d. www.python.com

Question 3

What is a variable?

a. An item that stores a value in the program.
b. An item that can change in value during the program.
c. This item is referenced by a certain name all throughout the program.
d. All of the above

Question 4

How do I create a random variable in Python?

a. Write numbers on a card and have your mom pick a card. Use that card to determine random value.
b. Use the rand() function in the random library in Python.
c. Toss a coin to add randomness to your program.
d. Take a shower before programming to inspire random thoughts.

Question 5

How do you calculate remainder in Python?

    a. Use the modulus sign %

    b. Use the division sign /

    c. Use the plus sign +

    d. Use the minus sign –

Question 6

What is an array in Python?

    a. An array is a group of variables.

    b. The variables are of the same data type.

    c. Each item in an array is referenced using an index.

    d. The first index in an array is 0.

    e. All of the above.

Question 7

What is a list in Python?

    a. An list is a group of variables.

    b. The variables can be of different data types.

    c. Each item in a list is referenced using an index.

    d. The reference index can be a string or number.

    e. All of the above.

Question 8

What is the difference between a list and an array?

    a. You have to write down a list on paper but can program an array.

    b. A list has a maximum number of items, but an array has unlimited number of items

    c. The reference index in an array is a number starting at 0, while the reference in a list can be a string or number.

    d. A list can have different data types while an array has items of the same data type.

    e. c and d above.

Question 9

Which Python is the best for creating drawings and animations?

   a. Math library
   b. Numpy library
   c. Turtle library
   d. Random library

Question 10

How do drawings work on Python library?

   a. Uses your dreams and imagination to locate a point and draw what you feel like is best.
   b. Draw an item on paper and take a picture. Then upload the picture, and Python will create a replica of it.
   c. Create a separate screen for the drawing.
   d. Uses a pen object that starts at a certain point and moves in a certain direction to a certain length.
   e. c and d above

Question 11

Create two integer variables called teamA and teamB and assign integer values to them representing the number of goals each team scored in a soccer game. Print out the values of each variable on the screen. Then, create a Boolean variable teamAWon to determine if Team A won the game, and print out the result using the Boolean value. Then, create a second Boolean called draw and check if the result is a draw.

Question 12

Create two variables to store the heights of two soccer players, named heightFriend1 and heightFriend2, respectively. Print their heights on the screen. Then, create a Boolean variable tallerFriend1 to figure out which player is taller, and print out the result using the Boolean value.

Question 13

Create two variables, player1 and player2, to store the names of two famous soccer stars. Create two integer variables, goals1 and goals2, to represent the number of goals they've scored. Print on the screen "Player 1 has x goals" and "Player 2 has y goals" using the four methods you've learned in the chapter "Printing Data onto a Screen in Python". Of course, you'd replace "Player 1" and "Player 2" with the actual names entered, and x and y with the actual number of goals scored.

Question 14

Write a program that takes in the value of your favorite stadium and prints it on the screen.

Question 15

Write a program that takes in the value of 10 soccer teams in your league and stores it in 10 different variables. Print out the teams at the end of the program.

Question 16

Create an array of 12 soccer teams with arrays containing the number of goals scored and goals conceded in a season. Calculate and print the team name and goal difference for the team.

Question 17

Create an array of 6 soccer stadiums with arrays containing the seating capacity and the city where each stadium is located. Print out the names of the stadiums along with their seating capacity and city.

Question 18

Create an array of 9 soccer players with distance covered in the season, and total number of games played. Calculate and print the distance covered per game for each player and also store the data in a third array.

Question 19

Create an array of 7 soccer players with their heights (in inches) and another array with their weights (in pounds). Print out the names of all players along with their height and weight.

Question 20

Create a Python program that draws the following shapes on the screen:

a. A horizonal blue line of size 3 in the top corner.

b. A vertical green line in the center of the screen of size 1.

c. A horizontal blue line in the bottom-right corner.

Question 21

Develop a Python script to draw 10 soccer balls in a horizontal row. The soccer balls are all of different colors.

Question 22

Create a Python program that draws a simple house on the screen. The house should have a brown rectangular base, a red triangular roof, and a yellow square window.

Question 23

Create a simple Python program that creates a circular soccer practice field with 10 soccer cones located anywhere on the circle. (Use dots for circles)

Question 24

Create a soccer ball animation where it checks if it hits the ground and stops the motion of the ball. (Check if the y-coordinate of the ball is below a horizontal line y-coordinate. You need to create a line for the ground, in addition to the ball)

Question 25

Using the code in the final chapter 'Moving a Soccer Ball on the Screen', create a second ball that moves using the keys **a,s,d** and **w**. This simulates a second player with a second ball. The key **a** is left, **d** is right, **w** is up and **s** is down. Make the ball color **'white'** so it stands out from the player one ball color.

Answers:

Answer 1 a)

Answer 2 c)

Answer 3 d)

Answer 4 b)

Answer 5 a)

Answer 6 e)

Question 7 e)

Question 8 e)

Question 9 c)

Question 10 e)

Conclusion / Next Steps

Thank you for taking the team to read this book.

I hope you had lots of fun and found it useful. If you've been through the exercises, you now understand the basics of Python, and able to program much more advanced applications in the future.

If you liked my book and you'd like to learn more, check out my Author page below. I'll have another book out soon that shows how to create a shopping cart from scratch using html, css and JavaScript.

https://www.amazon.com/Bob-Mather/e/B07HHQZC4Y

I'd also recommend looking at the other books in the section, especially the ones on how Artificial Intelligence will take over the world.

If you'd like any clarification regarding the topics; or any suggestions; please email me at: abiprod.pty.ltd@gmail.com

I also do one-one coaching online if you are interested in personalized help.

The end... almost!

Reviews are not easy to come by.

As an independent author with a tiny marketing budget, I rely on readers, like you, to leave a short review on Amazon.

Even if it's just a sentence or two!

So if you enjoyed the book, please click below and leave a review... I am very appreciative for your review as it truly makes a difference.

Thank you from the bottom of my heart for purchasing this book and reading it.

Printed in Great Britain
by Amazon